Hidden Power and False Expectations

Muted Group Theory for Urban Mission

Linda Lee Smith Barkman, PhD

Skyforest, CA | Urban Loft Publishers

Hidden Power & False Expectations
Muted Group Theory for Urban Mission

Copyright © 2020 Linda Lee Smith Barkman

All rights reserved. Except for brief quotations in critical publications or reviews, no part of this book may be reproduced in any manner without prior written permission from the publisher. Write: Permissions, Urban Loft Publishers, P.O. Box 6 Skyforest, CA, 92385.

Urban Loft Publishers
P.O. Box 6
Skyforest, CA 92385
www.urbanloftpublishers.com

Senior Editors: Stephen Burris & Kendi Howells Douglas
Track Editor: Joel Ickes
Graphics: Elisabeth Arnold

ISBN-13: 978-1-949625-09-7

Made in the U.S

*For Amy and Bethany,
and for Marge and my sisters at C. I. Wonderful.*

Table of Contents

Introduction 7
Chapter 1
   Background 11
Chapter 2
   What is Muted Group Theory? 17
Chapter 3
   Meet my friends! 39
Chapter 4
   What My Friends Teach Us About the Church 49
Chapter 5
   California Institution for Women: A Centered-Set Church ... 71
Chapter 6
   What My Friends Teach Us About Communication 91
Chapter 7
   What is Going on with Power? 111
Chapter 8
   Where does this leave MGT? 129
Chapter 9
   GSLC Case Study 159
Chapter 10
   Muted Group Theory and Urban Mission 177
A Concluding Story: Success 187
Appendix 193
Bibliography 201

Introduction

So how did I come to write a book at the intersection of urban mission, mass incarceration, and communication theory? The story begins with questions that troubled me as a prisoner at the California Institution for Women (CIW). However, these questions could not be answered until I had first experienced life outside of prison in a way that gave me a new perspective to these questions. Only then could the academic pursuit of understanding intercultural communication lead me to the answers.

I had already been incarcerated for fifteen or twenty years, and was considered an elder in the prison church, when I began to be very troubled by a pattern I observed repeating over and over again with women prisoners who were coming to Christ while in prison. It was particularly noticeable with short-termers (those serving less than three-year sentences). These women would ask Jesus into their lives with great joy and relief. There could be no question of whether or not their conversion was genuine because every aspect of their lives would be changing. These women would spend their every waking moment in church and Bible studies, in healthy Christian fellowship, or in reading their Bibles. The joy that emanated from them was palpable as they began to live lives that were free from the chains of sin. And when it came time for them to parole, they were so excited about the prospect of a new life in Jesus, leaning on the Scripture that says, "So if the Son makes you free, you will be free indeed" (John 8:36 NRSV). They would tell me "I have a church to go to outside and I just know I'll never come back to prison!"

All too often, within a few months this same sister in Christ would show up back in prison as a parole violator. Recidivism is an extreme problem in prison, so seeing women return was not a great shock. But what stood out about these women is how excited they were to return! It wasn't that they wanted to be incarcerated, but that they were so overjoyed to return to the church within the prison. Because I was an elder, because I was discipling some of these women, because I was teaching Bible studies with them, I felt some personal responsibility for what I was observing. What were we doing wrong as we prepared these women for life in the free world? What was wrong with the church in prison that caused women to come back instead of staying at home with their children and families? I had no idea. I, like most of the leaders in the prison church, was a long-termer who had never experienced parole. I only knew how church worked on the inside.

Years later, having paroled and completed a masters degree, I was still haunted by the memories of those women. I felt God's call to study further and began doctoral-level work. It was then, during a seminar where Dr. R. Daniel Shaw was guest lecturing, that I had the epiphany that has led to this book. Dr. Shaw was speaking about the church in Papua, New Guinea, and listing all the reasons that he considered this a thriving body of Christ. The church was growning. There was indigenous leadership. The gospel was being contextualized to meet the needs of the culture. This sounded just like the church at CIW. I suddenly realized that the issue was not the church in prison. According to Dr. Shaw's criteria, the church at CIW was doing things right! I realized that the true issue might be that the churches outside prison were not meeting the expectations of paroling women, something I had never previously conceptualized.

I then remembered a common exchange that, since I have been away from the prison for several years, I could now see from both sides. I would be in conversation with one of the outside prison ministry volunteers who had just experienced a prison church service for the first time, and the conversation would go something like this:

"Oh Linda! What a wonderful, Spirit-filled church service you have at CIW! I go to a really good church too, and you should visit us when you get out!"

I came to realize that what the sincere and loving volunteer was trying to communicate was that she felt the Spirit of God alive in our prison church the same way she experienced it at her church outside. But her reality is that the people in her church meet once or twice a week, for an hour or two, and worship together. They experience God's presence, and then they go home. And this experience was what she was intending to offer, and was all that she was intending to offer, to the women who would be leaving prison.

But what my sister prisoners were hearing was "Praise God! Your church is like mine at CIW! I can go to church seven days a week, and up to two or three times a day. There is always another believer within a hundred feet of me who understands all my problems and is able to pray with me at a moment's notice. No one judges me for my past. And all of my physical, emotional, and spiritual needs will be met. So as long as I spend all my time praying, reading the Bible, and fellowshipping with Christians, everything will be fine when I parole, because your church is like my church and will take care of me."

From whence did this disconnect come? Both sides of this exchange were speaking the same language, English. Both sides were being open and honest in the exchange. Moreover, both sides presumed that they were communicating effectively.

So it is within this milieu of U.S. subculture, within the dynamics that occur between prisoners and prison ministry volunteers at CIW, that this book will examine their communication using Muted Group Theory (MGT) as a framework. It is my hope and expectation that doing so will introduce MGT to urban mission practitioners in a manner that will not just explain these dynamics, but will make it possible to give voice to those who are powerless and marginalized, including prisoners.

Chapter 1

Background

Prison Ministry as Urban Mission

Mass incarceration in the U.S. is a current phenomenon that is relevant to every urban mission context. Over 2.1 million adults were held in American prisons and jails at the end of 2016, according to 2018 Bureau of Justice statistics, at a rate of 655 per 10,000 persons residing in the U.S.; if the incarcerated populated a city it would rate among the top 10 cities in the U.S.[1] I ask you to contemplate on the reality that this statistic only refers to those actually incarcerated. When the families, friends, and loved ones of those incarcerated are also considered, the number of persons directly affected by mass incarceration is staggering. Add to this picture that the non-white and poor are disproportionately represented in prisons and that crime rates are higher in urban contexts.

The looming threat of mass incarceration extends further, and in a way that especially intersects with urban youth. While police stops in New York City have increased over 600 percent in the last ten years, only ten percent of those contacts resulted in actual arrest or criminal charges, and a polling of young Americans revealed that twenty percent

---

[1] Drew Kann, "5 Facts Behind America's High Incarceration Rate," published April 21, 2019, CNN, https://www.cnn.com/2018/06/28/us/mass-incarceration-five-key-facts/index.html.

have been stopped and questioned by police.[2] Of course, these incidents affect marginalized minorities at a greater rate than white Americans, deepening "the divide between those Americans whose voice is heard and those whose views are silenced."[3]

These are the questions that this book will attempt to address: How it is that some voices are heard while others are silenced? What is the mechanism that underlies this dynamic? And what can be done about it? So while the case study and context of this work are seated in a California women's prison, anyone involved with urban mission will find this work relevant, both in terms of the issues of mass incarceration and in terms of how Muted Group Theory illuminates the dynamics of silencing the marginalized.

Background: The Toilet Tissue Church

I would like to share a story here that will serve to introduce you to my church at my prison, the way I experienced it. This is the story of how the Protestant church at the California Institution for Women (CIW) came to be known as "The Toilet Tissue Church."

The first-time prison ministry volunteers attend services at CIW they invariably are surprised to be handed a neatly folded rectangle of toilet tissue as they walk in the door.

"Why are you handing me toilet tissue?"

The inmate ushers hand one to each and every person entering the chapel. "Because we don't have Kleenex in prison."

---

[2] Amy E. Lerman and Vesla M. Weaver, "How Urban Policing and Mass Imprisonment Create a Second-Class Citizenship in America," Goldman School of Public Policy, UC Berkeley, June 17, 2014, https://gspp.berkeley.edu/research/featured/how-urban-policing-and-mass-imprisonment-create-a-second-class-citizenship.

[3] Ibid.

"But why do I need this in church?"

"Because when you are touched by the Holy Spirit and start to cry, you will need it."

At CIW the Protestant chaplain has significant power and authority to select which volunteer groups are given access to the prison. Sometime around 1988 a new chaplain was hired who, as a charismatic Baptist, opened up opportunities for Pentecostal churches to be better represented. In particular, on Sunday evenings a new group began to offer Protestant services. The group was an amalgam of Prison Fellowship volunteers from various churches, and a large pool of Vineyard Church musicians from John Wimber's Anaheim church. This service almost immediately became very popular, and the room that served as Protestant Chapel at that time was routinely filled beyond capacity for these services. For many women prisoners, this was their first introduction to Pentecostal worship.

Initially, when the women would begin to cry during these services, since facial tissues were unavailable, entire rolls of toilet tissue would be passed down the long rows of folding chairs to the women who were in need of it. However, this practice soon got out of hand. So many women were crying that toilet tissue rolls were being passed back and forth and back again throughout the entire service. It was disruptive in several ways: women who were trying to worship or listen were being interrupted, musicians and teachers were being distracted, and the flow of the interaction between the Holy Spirit and individual women was broken.

A simple solution slowly evolved. It became the job of the ushers to fold portions of toilet tissue into compact rectangles, and then to hand out these tissues to each and every person who entered the church...prisoner and volunteer alike. This is when some of the outside prison ministry volunteers started referring to the church at CIW as "The Toilet Tissue Church."

The toilet tissue ritual ultimately took on a life of its own. The passing out of toilet tissue became the common practice at all the Protestant services, including Spanish language services. The folding of the toilet tissue became a significant duty of all inmate ushers. Senior ushers passed on the ritual by instructing new ushers in the 'proper' manner for folding tissue. I have observed the great attention to detail given as precisely eight squares of tissue were pulled off the roll, folded in half, and again, and again, until the entire stack of small rectangles stood tall and even.

We took the toilet tissue ritual two steps further in the psychiatric unit services, which was a small and specialized congregation where I served as lay minister. The first step involved delivery method. The women with psychiatric concerns were less orderly in their comings and goings, and they frequently dropped their tissue on the floor. Therefore, we tucked the rectangle of tissue where it was just visible from under the cover of the worship songbook that was handed to each woman as she walked into the room where church was held. The second step involved the tissue itself. During the 1990s the prison store offered real Kleenex for sale. Although the price of one box was the equivalent of a half-day's wages, I personally bought and distributed real tissues. Eventually, however, Kleenex was determined to be such a luxury item that it was removed from the prison store inventory. Yet that last empty Kleenex box became the holder of the toilet tissue squares. When I paroled from CIW in 2010, we were still using that dilapidated box, held together with respect and tape.

How does this toilet tissue find its way to church? During flush times of prison economy, the chapel is allowed to requisition supplies from the warehouse. But often, procuring the tissue presents its own challenge. It is important to realize how valuable toilet tissue is in prison. Toilet tissue is a scarce commodity in a low-resource environment. Add to this that women prisoners use a lot of toilet tissue. Besides the obvious biological fact that women need and use more of it than men do, within CIW toilet tissue is the all-purpose paper product. Since access to napkins, paper towels, and facial tissue is limited or denied, toilet tissue serves all of these purposes. A pocket full of tissue serves for wiping hands and mouth during meals in the chow hall. Toilet tissue wipes up spills and cleans cell surfaces. A woman with serious allergies that cause burning eyes and runny nose can easily go through a roll of tissue a day.

Distribution of toilet tissue, especially because it is a scarce commodity, becomes a significant power dynamic in a woman's prison. Wardens, especially if a male warden is assigned to this facility, are known to limit access and ration toilet tissue for the sake of fiscal economy. I have heard male administrators explain, "I don't understand why you women are complaining, and why you are running out of toilet tissue. We are issuing you four rolls a week, and that is twice as much as we issue to the men!" Individual housing officers have been known to assert their power and control by rationing out rolls of toilet paper, locking supplies in a closet, and forcing women to stand in line to approach and request an additional roll of paper. Finally, the "house girls," women whose job it is to clean and run the living units, exert their own power and occasionally extort fellow prisoners, by controlling available commodities.

Toilet tissue is an important part of the prison economy. For those who could afford to purchase Kleenex when it was offered on canteen in the 1980s and 1990s, it was a symbol of wealth, luxury, and self-indulgence. There are periodic shortages of toilet tissue in the prison, especially at the end of the fiscal year when supplies and budgets are exhausted, but no purchases can be made until a state budget is confirmed. At times like these, women in educational programs are informed that the public restrooms in the education building are not being stocked with tissue and that they must bring their own. The inevitable hording is limited in part by a rule of no more than four rolls of toilet tissue allowed in each two-woman cell, which is enforced by periodic cell searches by staff. Prisoner clerks curry favor with prisoner warehouse workers in order to obtain a few extra rolls. During one particularly memorable toilet tissue shortage, two rolls of toilet tissue could be obtained on the prison black market in exchange for one pouch of rolling tobacco!

This was my church experience at CIW. When I refer to "church in prison," the Toilet Tissue Church is my mental image. And still, the above description does not fully evoke the depth of warmth, connection, and presence of God's Spirit that is also part of my experience at CIW.

Chapter 2

What is Muted Group Theory?

I ultimately discovered an explanation of why and how I come to be at a loss of words to describe the prison church in Muted Group Theory (MGT), but neither finding nor applying this explanation was simple. Early in my research I had read a line in a communication textbook about how MGT offered help in framing how the "language of the dominant cultural group contributes to the Microcultural group's subordination."[4] The discussion that followed related to how dominant groups find it more difficult to communicate with microcultural groups than the other way around, since microcultural group members need to learn macro group ways and rules in order to survive. Put another way, by another author, I read that, "Marginalized groups are not only forced to develop their own standpoints from a less privileged position but are also required to understand the standpoints of the more powerful" since a "slave must understand the master's standpoint to survive whereas the reverse cannot be said to be true."[5] This was enough to pique my

---

[4] James Neuliep, *Intercultural Communication: A Contextual Approach 7th ed.* (Thousand Oaks, CA: Sage, 2017), 97.

[5] Charlotte Krolokke and Anne Scott Sorenson, *Gender Communication Theories and Analysis: From Silence to Performance* (Thousand Oaks, CA: Sage, 2006), 32.

interest. It was certainly true in my experience that as a prisoner it was in my best interest to understand the language and perspectives of those who held power over me, while they had no interest in why and how circumstances had shaped my life.

Thus, I decided to take a deep look at what MGT was really about and whether it could provide a framework for my research. What I offer below is what I discovered, and then a bit more. So, in addition to the history and development of MGT, I add a nuanced definition of MGT and provide relevant examples of MGT at work. Finally, I expand upon MGT by contributing something new, a viable mechanism for promoting change.

History and Development of Muted Group Theory

The historical genesis of MGT is clear and well documented, originating within the discipline of anthropology. The husband-wife anthropological team of Edwin and Shirley Ardener coined the term "Muted Group Theory" in 1975.[6] Edwin Ardener, in looking for an explanation for why women's perspectives and voices were absent from anthropological studies, realized that women's voices were "often more 'inarticulate' than men, and thus pose special technical problems for the inquirer."[7] He suggested that women are disadvantaged in expressing matters of peculiar concern unless their views are presented either in a form acceptable to men and to "women brought up in the male idiom."[8] Edwin adopted the term "muted" over the word "inarticulate" in order

---

[6] Shirley Ardener, *Perceiving Women* (London: Malaby Press Limited, 1975) vii.
[7] Ibid., viii.
[8] Ibid., ix.

to counter some feminists' misunderstanding that he was referring to a biological condition of persons physically unable to make sound.[9]

To put MGT in historical context, its development was following on Marshall McLuhan's famous phrase regarding communication theory: "The medium is the message."[10] Thus, MGT claimed that it is not only the way that data is encoded into words by society that results in muting.[11] In fact, groups can be muted by the nature of discourse, even when the message of the discourse contradicts the medium.[12] For example, Shirley Ardener noticed that even when male anthropologists stated that they were taking women's voices seriously, women were often literally parenthesized, that is referred to as (or her) or (and wife).[13]

It is important to note that, although Edwin Ardener was looking at the predicament of women, he did not develop this theory in response to gender alone. His wife Shirley Ardener reminds us, "Edwin always maintained that muted group theory was not only, or even primarily, about women – although women comprised a conspicuous case in point."[14] In fact, it was Edwin's experiences in school as a scholastic youth (nerd) amongst more powerful athletic youths (jocks) that led him to conceive of the issues between dominant and subdominant groups. Therefore, while the first scholars to take up the discussion of MGT were feminists such as the American Kramarae, the

---

[9] Shirley Ardener, "Ardeners 'Muted Groups: the Genesis of an Idea and Its Praxis,'" *Women and Language,* 28, no. 2 (Fall 2005): 51.
[10] Marshall McLuhan, *Understanding Media: The Extensions of Man. Cambridge* (MA: MIT Press, 1964) 7.
[11] Ardener, "Muted Groups," 54.
[12] Ibid. 54.
[13] Ardener, "Muted Groups," 55.
[14] Ibid., 54.

Australian Spender, and the British Cameron, from its very conception, MGT was intended to be more than a gendered, feminist theory.[15]

In 1981 Cheris Kramarae, a scholar in the area of women's studies and communication, discovered in MGT a relevance to the field of communications.[16] Specifically, Kramarae noted that MGT informs the field of communication about how power functions in speech, writing, and language.[17] She made a serious contribution to gendered communication studies by introducing MGT, arguing that, since accepted language practices have been constructed primarily by men in order to express their experiences, women are thus muted.[18]

However, it is my intention to expand the role of MGT. Although the application of MGT to gendered communication is prominently featured, and validly so, I want to emphasize that MGT is not only, or even primarily a feminist tool. MGT explains communication dynamics whenever groups imbued with different power levels interact. I have also expanded the original three tenets of MGT to the five tenets presented here.

The original three address:
1) the issues of unequal participation in a society in generating and encoding ideas through language creation,
2) how the realities and values of the subdominant group are inadequately recognized and respected by the dominant group, and

---

[15] Ibid., 51.

[16] Cheris Kramarae, *Women and Men Speaking: Frameworks for Analysis* (New York: Newberry House Publishers, 1981) 59.

[17] Ibid., 55.

[18] Ibid., 55.

3) the mechanisms that limit access of the subdominant group to the arenas of power and policy where societal rewards are obtained.

To this list I add what others have considered implied instead of explicit, that these mechanisms can be resisted. Finally, and what I believes makes MGT such beneficial a tool for urban mission, I maintain that MGT theory applies not only to the interactions between the most dominant group and the rest as subdominant, but explains power dynamics between subgroups with micro-level power differences.

To further make evident the dynamic flow between the tenets of MGT, I have two personal examples that I will share in story form in association with each tenet.

Tenet #1 – Creating Language

The dominant group creates the language of power and policy based on their life experiences.

Because dominant and subdominant groups are afforded different life experiences, they perceive the world differently.[19] However, it is the dominant, more powerful group that is privileged to create language and define terms. These dominant and subdominant groups operate as "simultaneities," albeit there may be movement between membership in groups that are variously dominant and subdominant.[20] The language created and terms defined to describe

---

[19] Celia J. Wall and Pat Gannon-Leary, "A Sentence Made by Men: Muted Group Theory Revisited," *European Journal of Women's Studies* 6 (1): 21-29.

[20] Ardener, "Muted Groups," 52.

the life experiences of the dominant group are not therefore adequate to describe the life experiences of the subdominant group.

Example: I recently was hired to do some consulting work. My Japanese-American male teammate and I were asked to prepare an online training module for faculty who were preparing to teach college classes within prisons for the first time. We included a section titled "Guidelines for Manipulation by Students" in which we stressed that manipulation is a survival skill for prisoners. Our work was reviewed by an outside panel of white male college professors, who strongly objected to our use of the word "manipulation," saying, "It is just wrong!" We were directed to modify our language.

Tenet #2 - Muting

The dominant group's life experiences differ from the subdominant group's life experiences, which leads to the muting of the subdominant group.

So while the subdominant group may create language and define terms to describe its life experiences, the subdominant group's modes of expression are less acceptable to and less respected by the dominant group.[21] This is especially true concerning the language of power and policy. The focus of MGT is on the way language names experiences and therefore determines which facets of social and individual meanings and behaviors are recognized and respected.[22]

---

[21] Wall and Gannon-Leary, "A Sentence Made by Men," 26.

[22] Maria T. Allison and Dan Hibbler, "Organizational Barriers to Inclusion: Perspectives from the Recreation Professional," *Leisure Sciences* 26 (3): 265, doi: 10.1080/01490400490461396.

Example: What the members of the reviewing panel were really saying is "We white men are not subject to the kind of manipulation you are referencing and besides, we have determined that it is politically incorrect to use that kind of language." While the dominant men who wrote the response do have experience teaching classes in prisons, they have only done so in the lowest security, male-only facilities, that do not house prisoners with violent records or behavior problems. On the other hand, our personal experience is with high security, with male and female prisons, and where the consequences that result from manipulation are much greater and where the repercussions are more serious when boundaries are crossed. Still, the end result was that our experiences were discounted by the reviewing panel, who directed us to change our wording. We were muted.

Tenet #3 – Consequences

Subdominant group members must either learn to use the dominant group language or suffer the loss of societal benefits.

Therefore, the subdominant groups must use the dominant mode of communication, either translating into the dominant mode of expression or becoming bilingual and speaking in both modes.[23] This can be described as a form of cultural imperialism, when all points of reference are normalized and centered within the dominant experience, while the voices of non-dominant individuals and groups are minimized, stigmatized, or muted.[24]

---

[23] Wall and Gannon-Leary, "A Sentence Made by Men," 26.
[24] Allison and Hibbler, "Organizational Barriers to Inclusion," 264.

Example: My teammate and I each have advanced degrees in communication. We were able to use academic language to justify to our direct supervisors why they should not remove the material the review panel had issues with. We were able to adequately argue that, while the panel members thought that they were protecting prisoners, our insider experiences were to the contrary. In fact, as a former prisoner, I felt threatened by their naïve attitude. If we had not been able to respond in dominant group language, we would have remained muted, the college programs would be likely jeopardized by poorly trained outside faculty, and subdominant group prisoner/students could as a result lose this educational opportunity.

Tenet #4 – Resistance and Change

Resistance and change are possible!

Although not explicitly named by Ardener or Kramarae, some scholars have recognized what they call a critical, if unstated, fourth tenet. I assert that this fourth tenet is an integral and vital component of MGT; resistance and change are possible.[25] This possibility of resistance and change is what keeps MGT from being a pessimistic labeling of the marginalized and instead turns MGT into an optimistic tool for providing hope and voice to the marginalized. However, MGT does not merely state that change and resistance are possible. MGT also provides the tools, by explaining the process of muting, that allow confronting and resisting the muting of marginalized groups and persons.

---

[25] Mary Meares et al., "Employee Mistreatment And Muted Voices In The Culturally Diverse Workplace." *Journal of Applied Communication Research* 32 (1):4-27.

Example: What my teammate and I are trying to do is to acquaint the new faculty to the subdominant language and culture of prison. Our immediate supervisor heard our argument and decided to side with us over the reviewing panel; their muting of us did not stand. This is our attempt to resist the dominant group and affect the perspectives of new faculty.

Tenet #5 – Microcultural Differences; a Mechanism for Change

Microcultural power differences exist and are vital in providing a mechanism for resistance and change.

My research shows that MGT dynamics are at work even when the power differential between groups is minimal. Groups that are slightly more powerful still have enough dominance to mute subdominant group members who are just slightly less powerful. It is for this reason that we must pay attention to micro power differentials not only in the mission field, but also in the mission effort. By this I mean that the power differentials that exist in the sending organization and between the various field workers also result in muting dynamics.

Example: My teammate, as a Japanese-American male, is only a small increment less powerful than the Academic Senate leaders. Additionally, we are both very close to equal in power with our project supervisor, who hired us as outside experts. Yet even with this very small power differential between us and those we were working with, we found ourselves enmeshed in MGT power dynamics in order to avoid being muted.

MGT as a Gendered Theory

Historically, MGT has unfortunately only been found discussed in the gender section of undergraduate communication texts, where it hides as one more incomplete theory of gendered communication issues.[26] However, those who relate MGT only to gendered communications have gravely misperceived both the intention and appropriate application of this theory.

Yet MGT does make important contributions to understanding gendered communications. Some critics have pointed out deficiencies in MGT in accounting for gender differences in communications.[27]

A quick search on YouTube reveals a number of undergraduate presentations on MGT for communication classes where MGT only pertains to macro-level power dynamics, usually gender-based.[28] However, I reiterate that MGT was never intended to be primarily about gender (Ardener 2005, 51), and gender is a complex issue that involves more than power dynamics. MGT is about power dynamics; it is relationships, not the situations, which are responsible for muting voices.[29] Understanding the processes of dominance and muting requires a broader analysis of the context – political, economic, and

---

[26] Scott A. Chadwick, "Contexts of Communication," accessed 3/4/16. http://oregonstate.edu/instruct/theory/mutedgrp.html; Neuliep, *Intercultural Communication*, 97.

[27] D. Vasanta, "Researching Language and Gender: A Critical Review," *Indian Journal of Gender Studies* 8 (1): 69-87. doi: 10.1177/097152150100800104; Wall and Gannon-Leary, *A Sentence Made by Men*, 27.

[28] Rachel Johnson, "Muted Group Theory – The Film," [YouTube], https://www.youtube.com/watch?v=_beiMIQm_OA; Elise Sanders et al., "Steinheimer Incorporated - Muted Group Theory." [YouTube], https://www.youtube.com/watch?v=o0zMkIegMpY.

[29] Ardener, "Muted Groups," 51; Rachel Lepchitz, "Perceived Muted Voice and its Impact on Female Communication Techniques in the Workplace." (MA Unpublished Thesis, Communication and Leadership Studies, Gongaza University, 2012), 50.

institutional – in which reality is negotiated.[30] It is true that MGT does not account for all linguistic gender differences. However, this is not a fatal flaw. MGT does indeed still contribute understanding to some gender differences, even though this is not the primary intention of this theory.

Celia Wall and Pat Gannon-Leary answer the charge that MGT fails to acknowledge the fact that women do speak publicly with the observation that the concept of male/female arena division has been discredited and that "separate spheres are rarely truly separate."[31] I am even less concerned about this charge because MGT does in fact account for the fact that the subdominant group may speak, but that the language of the dominant group must be used for that speech to be recognized and respected. I experienced this myself when, as a first-year PhD student, I found myself being graded down for written use of language that my male TAs considered "not academic" but that I recognized was how women speak. What I did not recognize at that time was the reality that, even though I had consciously chosen to not use forms and vocabulary that were associated with my prison enculturation, I was unconsciously using precisely those forms and vocabulary. I have subsequently become more proficient in using the language of the dominant group in order to have my voice heard within academia.

Further, while for the most part in the U.S., women are a subdominant group and men form a dominant group, not all men are always members of dominant groups. For example, power roles are reversed when the man is a prisoner and the woman is a Correctional

---

[30] Wall and Gannon-Leary, *A Sentence Made by Men*, 27.
[31] Wall and Gannon-Leary, *A Sentence Made by Men*, 26.

Officer. MGT allows for and explains these apparent contradictions, accounting for the fact that no one group is always dominant and sometimes marginalized members participate in dominating other groups as a result of hegemonic process.[32]

While some users of MGT may neglect the complex nature of gender, class, and race domination, a great strength of MGT is that the theory itself respects the complexities of cultural differences.[33] Wall and Gannon-Leary, upon revisiting MGT in 1999, found it to still be relevant and applicable beyond the gender-based.[34] Carol Colfer suggests that "valuable information and perspectives" are possessed by muted groups, which in the business world can be of aid in planning and building effective programs.[35]

MGT is a tool for engaging with the various levels at which dominance and subdominance defines groups and affects the ability of persons to effectively articulate their life experiences. In this way MGT accounts for the power dynamic that results in muting between groups of women where the dominant group does not even recognize that they are dominant.

Feminist Standpoint Theory

Feminist Standpoint Theory (FST) is frequently linked to MGT in academic literature.[36] Both theories focus on providing voice to the

---

[32] Meares et al., "Employee Mistreatment," 8.

[33] Cheris Kramarae, "Muted Group Theory and Communication: Asking Dangerous Questions." *Women and Language* 28 (2): 58.

[34] Wall and Gannon-Leary, *A Sentence Made by Men*, 26.

[35] Carol J. Pierce Colfer, "On communication Among 'Unequals,'" *International Journal of Intercultural Relations* 7 (3): 267.

[36] Allison and Hibbler, "Organizational Barriers to Inclusion,"; Kramarae, "Muted Group Theory,"; Consolata Nthemba Mutua, "Opposite Worlds, Singular Mission: Teaching as an ITA." New Directions for Teaching & Learning 2014 (138): 51-60. doi: 10.1002/tl.20096.;

marginalized.[37] FST is interested in the ways that language, culture and politics function as "prisonhouses of conventional knowledge" in a way that is closely related to MGT.[38] Both MGT and FST recognize the hierarchical structure of society that results in some groups being dominant over others.[39] Both also recognize and value the knowledge and lives of subdominant groups. In fact, a subdominant group's knowledge may reflect reality more closely than that of the dominant group.[40] And both are political, although MGT is more concerned with the politics of naming and FST more concerned with the politics of designating social groups.[41]

However, MGT and FST are still distinctly different in two major ways. First, MGT focuses on language and the power of naming while FST focuses on knowledge and how this knowledge is structured by power relations.[42] The second difference entails the point of view involved; while MGT looks to the social landscape to see and hear the groups being described, FST listens to the labels used by individuals to describe their own places.[43] This is because FST entails conscious knowledge of and struggle against the dominant group worldview. One

---

Richard L. West and Lynn H. Turner, "*Introducing Communication Theory: Analysis and Application, 2nd Ed.*" In: McGraw-Hill Higher Education Online Resources (accessed 1/29/16); Wood, Julia T. 2005. "Feminist Standpoint Theory and Muted Group Theory: Commonalities and Divergences." Women and Language 28 (2): 61-65

[37] Mutua, "Opposite Worlds," 53.

[38] Kramarae, "Muted Group Theory," 58.

[39] Allison and Hibbler, "Organizational Barriers to Inclusion," 266.

[40] Anne Johnston, Barbara Friedman and Sara Peach, "Standpoint in Political Blogs: Voice, Authority, and Issues." *Women's Studies* 40 (3): 269-298. doi: 10.1080/00497878.2010.548427, 291.

[41] Wood, "Feminist Standpoint Theory," 63.

[42] Ibid.

[43] Kramarae, "Muted Group Theory," 58.

must consciously choose to attain a standpoint.[44] MGT's position is in sharp contrast, where not only does one not consciously choose to be muted, but due to the lack of language to describe life experiences, muted group members may not even recognize that they are muted.[45]

Co-cultural Theory

Co-cultural theory is Mark Orbe's attempt to integrate MGT and standpoint theory in order "to shed light on the various ways in which persons reinforce, manage, alter, and overcome a societal position that renders them outside the centers of power."[46] Orbe refers to subdominant groups such as women, gays, bisexuals and persons of color as co-cultural groups.[47] He argues his preference for the term 'co-cultural groups' due to a connotation of static positionality in the term 'muted group.'[48] I appreciate that co-cultural theory is useful in helping scholars to understand that there is no single definitive form of communication for any specific co-culture.[49] However, I do not find this corollary theory to be either as useful for my purposes or as universally applicable as MGT.

---

[44] Wood, "Feminist Standpoint Theory," 63.

[45] Jean Mills, "Talking about silence: Gender and the construction of multilingual identities." *International Journal of Bilingualism* 10 (1):1-16. doi: 10.1177/13670069060100010101, 4.

[46] Allison and Hibbler, "Organizational Barriers to Inclusion," 266.; Mark P. Orbe, "Continuing the Legacy of Theorizing From the Margins: Conceptualizations of Co-Cultural Theory." *Women and Language, 2005*, 28 (2): 65-66,72. It is ironic that in Orbe's first contact with MGT, his professor effectively muted him by disallowing MGT as a project topic (Orbe 2005). I suspect his perspective on muted group implying a static position, and his therefore preferring to give the name co-cultural, has to do with gender power differentials and that different nondominant groups differently experience the static/fluid boundaries of dominance.

[47] Allison and Hibbler, "Organizational Barriers to Inclusion," 262.

[48] Orbe, "Continuing the Legacy," 66.

[49] Ibid.

How do the Muted Respond?

In their article, Meares et al. advanced MGT through research that has revealed that there are three types of muted response.[50] People who are muted generally fall into one of the following three categories: (1) muted but engaged, (2) angrily disengaged, and (3) resigned. Their research was done in the context of business and mistreatment of employees, but their results reach beyond this immediate context.[51] In accepting their assumption that it is reasonable to equate muting with mistreatment, their grouping of responses is applicable to other muted groups.

Muted But Engaged

Muted but engaged: The subdominant group member experiences muting but continues to attempt to communicate. Engagement allows the muted both to (a) learn the language of the dominant in order to reap societal benefits, and (b) resist and possibly change the dominant society. Muted but engaged persons remain constructive and have not given up trying to work through the system, despite their frustrations from neither being heard nor receiving a response from the dominant group.[52]

As a prisoner, I had to learn the language of CDCR, and either remain engaged or become institutionalized. As a parolee, I did not even know the language at my church. What IS a narthex? I'd never heard the word before. And what they considered worship was not what I was used to. As a new PhD student, I was told my writing was not quite

---

[50] Meares et al., "Employee Mistreatment," 13.
[51] Ibid.
[52] Ibid., 13-14.

"academic" enough by my male TA. I tried to explain that I was using women's language, but that explanation had no meaning for him.

Angrily Disengaged

Angrily Disengaged: The subdominant group member experiences muting but, due to frustration, no longer attempts to continue communication. Angrily disengaged persons focus on anger, when their agency is limited, in order to avoid the situation or the mistreater.[53] Reaction to muting is thus to physically withdraw.[54]

Attempting to communicate with those who are not listening is profoundly frustrating and dehumanizing. However, if the muted person gives up and stops trying, there is no chance of achieving a communication breakthrough with the muter. Additionally, the underlying anger that arises from frustration is frequently off-putting to those with whom the muted person is attempting to communicate, and provides further excuse for the muter to dismiss what the subdominant person says as irrelevant. When I remember the Watts riots of 1965, I wonder how many of the rioters were angrily disengaged persons who could no longer tolerate both being muted and being denied societal benefits.

I did not find any of my FIW friends to exhibit signs of being angrily disengaged persons. I suspect this is so for at least the following two related reasons. First, angrily disengaged prisoners are not likely to be deemed suitable for parole by the parole board, since they perceived anyone exhibiting hostility as possibly dangerous and a threat to society.

---

[53] Ibid., 15.
[54] Ibid., 16.

Second, an angrily disengaged FIW would be less motivated to invest the time and energy needed to participate in this study.

Resigned Response

Resigned Response: Resigned response is the far end of the disengagement continuum. It is an extension of angrily disengaged, but here no optimism that change is possible remains for the muted persons, who therefore become resigned and apathetic.[55]

There can be no change if the muted person has withdrawn and left the conversation. I do know of at least one apathetic and withdrawn FIW who paroled; she is not seen as a threat by the powerful since she is not resisting them. However, even when subdominant group members are resigned to not being heard, MGT provides an understanding that could result in dominant group members learning to recognize that muting has occurred, with the potential outcome of their learning to hear, accept, and respect the different experiences of subdominant group members.

One More Example: Muted Group Theory at Work

Going through the PhD dissertation process almost did me in; the experience was psychologically and emotionally brutal. What made it worse was that I was experiencing muting in interactions with the very persons I desperately needed to convince to approve my work on muting! This is what the experience looks like when viewed through the lens of MGT.

Tenet #1: I tried to explain to my committee members, all white educated people, that appearing before their tribunal felt a lot like

---

[55] Meares et al., "Employee Mistreatment," 16-17.

appearing before the Board of Parole Hearings (BPH) panel. They kept insisting that the two were nothing alike. After all, they each assured me, this committee was for my benefit, and everyone was on my side. They promised they would be gentle and respectful as they tried to guide me through my dissertation research problem approval. Although it was technically possible that I could be dropped from the PhD program if this meeting was not successful and they did not approve of my research idea and plan, such was beyond unlikely to almost impossible.

Tenet #2: But these kind and loving people had no idea what a BPH hearing was like, so they could not imagine any negative impact I might experience. From my perspective, BPH hearings were the single most important event in my annual cycle of life in prison. It was a tribunal of powerful, educated, and usually white, people who held my entire future in their hands. They were not always adversarial. In the last decade of my incarceration, I had actually been granted parole at every hearing, only to have that decision reversed by the sitting governor each time until 2010. Still, in these hearings I was required to tear open all of my emotional and psychological wounds, and parade my deepest shame and pain, in order to show my remorse for my crime. I was not allowed to emphasize that it was someone else who had killed my child, because that would not be taking responsibility for the crime for which I had been sent to prison. Although the law required the BPH to consider Battered Woman Syndrome in their findings, I was not really allowed to focus on this because, again, I would then be minimizing my involvement in the crime for which I had been convicted and sentenced.

In both cases, with the BPH and with the committee, the societal benefits that were at risk should I not communicate well in the dominant language were extreme. The BPH panel had the power to keep me incarcerated for the rest of my life if they so chose. The dissertation committee could deem my studies to be of no value, and thus deny me a subsequent career based on the results of my dissertation research. For both I found myself in a situation where I had to speak clearly, soulfully, in the language of the dominant, or else forfeit all of my dreams and aspirations.

The most memorable moments of that dissertation hearing involved a discussion of how I was going to collect my research materials. One member insisted that, in order to collect relevant data about prisoners I would have to obtain entry to the prison and interview prisoners in person. I explained that, because I was still on parole at that time, I would need special clearance from the Warden, and that the prison administrative staff had suffered sufficient turnover that there was no one remaining who knew me well enough to speak on my behalf. My powerful white male professor's answer to this was, "I will talk to the seminary president, and have him write a letter to the governor on your behalf, asking for him to directly give you permission to re-enter the prison." He was quite pleased with having come up with such a promising way to support me in my studies.

And then I explained to him, "Please listen to what you are saying to me. I spent decades trying to get out of prison. I was granted parole at eleven different BPH hearings, just to have their decision overturned by the sitting governor the first ten times. And your solution to my dissertation problem is to ask the governor to send me back to prison?" His face fell, horrified, as he began to understand.

Resistance and change are possible, but at this juncture I did not have a mechanism to help my committee, who were on my side, to understand the process of muting. The woman on my committee, who had experienced being muted as a woman in a man's milieu, supported my focus on MGT as framework for my research. She did not understand prison, but she absolutely could identify with the concept of muting. The white man however, in an ironic twist, believed that Relevance Theory of Communication was, well, more relevant. It appeared that MGT was going to suffer muting once again. So I read up on both theories, presented a formal academic argument elucidating my reasons for choosing MGT over Relevance Theory, and was allowed to continue my research. I had learned dominant language and was able to communicate effectively enough in it to avoid losing societal benefits. This was the only resistance mechanism that I could imagine.

I passed my dissertation defense with "distinction," and was acknowledged to have "advanced" MGT as a theory. In particular, I had contributed proof that MGT described dynamics that were present even when the power differential between the dominant group and the subdominant group was very small. It was almost a year later before I realized how important this contribution is, that within this discovery lies the secret to influencing the dominant group to embrace change.

Change never comes easily. I had a sense that what was necessary to bring a dominant group person to resist muting others was compassion, an understanding that the other had been wronged and been caused pain. However, compassion is difficult to attain without some level of commonality of experience. I had been asked to speak at a couple of venues where I would be presenting MGT to a mostly dominant group (white American male) audience; how could I find an example that they could relate to? I needed to find a situation in which they had been subdominant, something that was possible now that micro-level power differences were proved to still result in MGT dynamics with the muting of the subdominant. There are subgroups within the category of "white males" of varying power levels. By tapping into these situations, I could make the concept of muting "relevant" to those formerly always considered to be dominant group members. Absolutely every adult has experienced being a less dominant adolescent. So by making the concept of muting relevant, compassion for the muted was possible. And where compassion exists, this can be developed into the motivation to resist and change.

In this example, over time, change did occur. My male committee member became enthusiastic about my work and MGT. He already had a compassionate heart, and slowly I was able to present him with examples to which he could relate. The latest development is this man, who was so invested in Relevance Theory, is now referring his PhD students to my work with MGT.

Chapter 3

Meet my friends!

Initially, I had hoped to return to my prison, the California Institution for Women (CIW) in order to interview some of those short-term prisoners who were so happy to return to their home church there, and to reconnect with Prison Ministry Volunteers (PMVs) I had known. However, the same circumstance that made me the right person to conduct this research made it impossible for me to proceed in such a manner; as someone who had been incarcerated at CIW, I needed the Warden's permission to set foot on prison grounds. The problem was that, in the several years since I had walked out of those prison gates at CIW, the entire administration of the prison had changed, and no one remained who knew me and was willing to vouch for me. Ironically, I was unable to obtain permission to reenter the prison. So, instead, I reached out to my friends.

How I Found My friends, the Formerly Incarcerated Women (FIW)

My original study parameters called for FIW subjects who had served two-year terms or less, but it became quickly apparent that locating and contacting such a subject pool was prohibitively difficult.

There are several reasons for this. First of all, short-term prisoners have a high recidivism rate, which means that many of them return to prison quickly and are not available as subjects. Secondly, due to the shorter duration of their incarceration, short-termers make fewer long-term relationships with other prisoners, and are therefore more likely to simply leave prison behind. As one long-termer FIW put it when I asked if she knew of any paroled short-termers, "They disappear into the woodwork, never to be seen again." But the most serious limitation was that, since I did not have access to the prison, I did not have an insider to refer possible subjects to me.

I thus decided to base my study on lifer and long-termer FIWs who had been released after serving their sentences. I had maintained contact with a modest number of the women I had known during my own incarceration at CIW. Therefore, I decided to use a method

Choosing Which Group is Normative

A central focus of my study is power dynamics between dominant and subdominant groups, which according to Muted Group Theory (MGT) results in the muting of the subdominant group. In an effort to resist further muting the subdominant FIWs, I decided to turn the tables, quite literally. I made a deliberate decision to compare Prison Ministry Volunteers (PMVs) to FIWs in my tables and examples throughout this work. I am making FIWs the normative group against which the PMVs are compared and contrasted. This arrangement is counter-intuitive since usually the dominant group is presented as normative and the subdominant group is examined for its degree of deviance. In this dynamic, even the word "deviance" is pejorative.

One example of how this plays out occurs when measuring academic success rates of ethnic minority students to determine equity. The ethnic minority scores are compared and contrasted to the scores of the white majority students. The white student group is thus the (normative) dominant group and provides the standard by which the (deviant) minority groups are thus rated.

called snowball sampling. Snowballing is a chain-referral method where initial subjects serve as "seeds" through which waves of recruits are found and the sample grows in subsequent layers like a snowball rolling downhill. It is a convenient method for researchers whose exclusive concern is accessing "hidden populations," in this case FIWs.[56]

In addition to having served a life term or long term at CIW, I was looking for FIWs who had committed their lives to Christ either during their incarceration or immediately preceding, and who lived within a 150-mile radius of the California Institution for Women (CIW). My FIW friends had established and maintained a network of connections such that, through snowballing, I was ultimately able to recruit seventeen subjects who met these criteria for inclusion in this study. This number includes two FIWs who had been deported upon parole and were currently residing in Tijuana, Mexico. Of these seventeen, I determined during the interview process that one FIW did not fit the study parameters (she had in fact always been committed to Christ). Another FIW withdrew due to anxiety issues triggered by talking about prison. Therefore, this study is based on fifteen FIW subjects.

One important issue that needs to be addressed here involves the nature of my relationships with the FIWs as research subjects. I had long-term pre-existing relationships with each and every FIW subject. It could not be avoided. We had been encapsulated within the same community of less than 2,000 women for a period of between six and thirty years. Two of these women had each, for a period of time, shared a cell with me. I was therefore initially concerned that my close

---

[56] Douglas D. Heckathorn, "Snowball versus Respondent-Driven Sampling." *Sociological Methodology*, 2011, 41 (1): 355.

relationships would be a liability, causing my data to be deemed less reliable. I am therefore greatly indebted to the writings of the esteemed late Ada Maria Isazi-Diaz.[57] This woman theologian clarified in her study of the theologies of Latina women, the difference between using and abusing subjects when the researcher is both an insider and an outsider. Replace her term "Latinas" with "Formerly Incarcerated Women" and she describes my relationship with my FIW subjects:

> Of course, there is some "using" involved in the theological process I have been describing, a "using" that I believe is part of the give-and-take of relationships. So, the issue is not "using" but "abusing." Concerning this issue, consider the following. In my dealings with grassroots Latinas I am an insider/outsider. I am an insider insofar as I share religious understandings and practices, insofar as I too am marginalized and oppressed in the USA precisely because I am a Latina. I am an outsider mainly because of economic status and schooling. And, as an outsider, of course I am concerned about "using" in an oppressive way, about "abusing" grassroots Latinas. Certain things help in this regard. In our conversations I always attempt to have a reciprocal exchange of information. As an interviewer I participate in the process and do not understand myself merely as a listener, as an observer. I answer the questions; I share what I believe and how I try to live out those beliefs.
>
> Another point to consider here is this: because I and others with whom I work are in many ways insiders to the community being researched, in mujerista theology we have Latinas researching Latinas. This means that the "researched" are, to a certain extent, in charge of the process.[58]

---

[57] Ada Maria Isasi-Diaz, *La Lucha Continues: Mujerista Theology*, (Maryknoll, NY: Orbis Books, 2004), 5.

[58] Ada Maria Isasi-Diaz, *La Lucha Continues*, 5.

I too, am an insider and outsider. If I am an outsider due to my privilege as a highly educated white woman, I am also, in a very literal sense, an insider who shares the designation FIW.

Another important element of my interview methodology concerns why I continued transcribing the last three FIW interviews. After completing the first dozen interviews; I had already reached the point where I was no longer receiving new answers to the questions I was asking. As anyone who has ever transcribed verbal conversations knows, this is a tedious and difficult job. For every hour of recording it takes four to five times as long to transcribe. However, I discovered that as a result of my experiences with the prior interviews, my interviewing technique had so improved that I elicited much stronger and clearly stated responses in the later interviews, especially to some of the most pertinent questions in these latter interviews. I therefore transcribed and included these three particularly important and relevant interviews.

How I Found My Friends, the Prison Ministry Volunteers (PMVs)

PMVs were recruited using a combination of methods. There were those PMVs who were personally known to me and, upon being contacted, were willing to participate in this study. However, reestablishing contact with PMVs that I had known during my incarceration presented its own challenge. PMVs are not allowed to have contact with women they met within the prison who are subsequently on parole. Any contact that is made, such as a chance meeting at a store or restaurant, must be reported to prison authorities. The rational for this policy is to prevent over-familiarity between prisoners and volunteers. So although I was no longer on parole, I did not initially have direct contact information.

It was finally through extensive internet search and subsequent email contact with known prison ministry groups such as Prison Fellowship that I was able to locate a few old friends. I then relied on the snowballing technique described above. One PMV in particular, who had volunteered for eighteen years as assistant to the staff Protestant Chaplain, was a goldmine of referrals. It was the CIW Protestant Chaplain herself who referred the last PMV subject. I ultimately recruited and interviewed twenty PMVs; however, I only used nineteen as subjects.

I am so grateful to my first interview subject, Donna, whose data is not included in this study.[59] This initial interview was problematic and never completed due to my inexperience. Donna was exceptionally patient with me even when I could not adequately express what I was asking for. I learned much during this process, but decided to consider Donna's interview a pilot study and did not include it in the study.

In an unexpected bonus, CIW's Protestant Chaplain, volunteered to be interviewed as a part of my study. My FIW friend Julie, as we were concluding our interview session, asked me if I had contacted the Chaplain yet. Upon hearing that I had not, Julie immediately called the Chaplain, told her about my research, and asked if she would be willing to be interviewed. To my surprise, the Chaplain said she would be delighted. It is impossible to disguise the Chaplain's identity, since there is only one staff Protestant Chaplain at CIW. I explained this to her, on the record, and her response was to give me permission to use

---

[59] This is a pseudonym, as are most names used in this work. The exceptions, where actual names are used, are at the expressed request and permission of the subject.

identifiers and even her name. I decided to simply refer to her as "Chaplain" throughout this study.

What My Friends Tell Us About Themselves

In order to collect information from my friends, I conducted semi-structured interviews. This data collection technique is specifically recommended for qualitative study regarding lived experiences, for understanding how people understand and experience their world.[60] (Bernard 2011, 158; Kvale 2007, 9). Interviews were held at a time and location that was convenient for each subject. For some this meant I was invited into their homes, for others it meant meeting in a restaurant or coffee shop, while for yet others it meant inviting them to my home.

In addition to a script of prewritten interview questions, I also had prepared three written activities that I presented at some point during each interview: a Pile Sort, a Likert Scale, and a Semantic Differential. Each of these will be explained in detail as the data and results are discussed later.

What My Friends the FIWs Tell Us About Themselves

The Formerly Incarcerated Women (FIWs) subject pool consists of fifteen women, all of whom I knew from my own incarceration at the California Institution for Women (CIW) from 1980 to 2010. Thirteen had served life-term sentences at CIW and were considered "lifers," serving an average of 25 years. The remaining two, while serving six years each, had been actually sentenced to seven or more years, which is the prison

---

[60] H. Russell Bernard, *Research Methods in Anthropology: Qualitative and Quantitative Approaches, fifth edition*. NY, NY: Rowman & Littlefield, 2011; Steinar Kvale, *Doing Interviews*, Edited by Uwe Flick, The Sage Qualitative Research Kit, Los Angeles, CA: SAGE, 2007.

criteria to be considered a "long termer." Although one woman had transferred to another California prison in the middle of serving her sentence, the other fourteen served their entire sentences at CIW. The FIWs had all been converted or dedicated to Christ either sometime during or immediately preceding their incarceration in the time span from 1984 to 2010.

The age of FIWs ranged from 49 to 73 with an average age of 56 years. While incarcerated at CIW, the FIWs weekly attendance at Protestant church services ranged from two to thirty-five hours per week, with an average of 11.4 hours. Including the four FIWs who do not currently attend any church services, the average church attendance by FIWs is 8.8 hours per week. While one FIW attends 30 hours per week, the average participation in church services, excluding those who do not attend church at all, is 12 hours per week.

Pertinent demographic information regarding the Chaplain is that she is female, African-American, ordained African Methodist Episcopal, and worked as Protestant Chaplain at CIW for 20 years prior to her retirement in January 2019.

What My Friends the PMVs Tell Us About Themselves

Before beginning the formal interview, I asked each person to fill out a demographic survey, from which the following data was compiled. The Prison Ministry Volunteers (PMVs) subject pool consists of fourteen women and five men. While two PMVs are in their thirties, the remainder range in age from fifty-three to seventy-five years old. Sixteen PMVs self-identify as white/Caucasian. Of the remaining three, two self-identify as black/African-American and the third as multi-ethnic African-Native American. Of the first fourteen PMV subjects referred, all but one are white women. I began overtly requesting referrals to males and ethnic minorities. No Hispanic PMVs responded to my requests. Ultimately, five men, two of whom are African-American, responded and participated in this study.

Self-identified denominational affiliations include ten non-denominational, seven Calvary Chapel, two First Evangelical Free, and one Seventh Day Adventist. Of the two Pentecostal PMVs, one crossed out Pentecostal and wrote Non-denominational, verbally explaining that Pentecostal was too controversial. The other left this section of the survey blank, but revealed during his interview that he had been directed by a previous chaplain to refrain from Pentecostal expressions of healing ministry at the California Institution for Women (CIW).

The age of PMVs ranged from 34 to 75 with an overall average age of 59 years old. While one man and the only non-Caucasian woman are in their thirties, none of the PMVs was in their forties, so an adjusted average that does not include these two is 62 years of age. The PMVs range of years ministering at CIW range from 1 to 44, with an average of 12 years. The number of hours per month that the PMVs volunteer at CIW range from 1 to 40, with an average of 11.4 hours. The number of hours per week that PMVs attend their own churches on the outside range from 1 to 8, with an average of 3.8 hours. If the number of hours the PMVs minister at CIW is combined with the number of hours they attend services in their own churches, the adjusted average is 6.5 hours per week. This is just over half the number of hours that the FIWs who attend church report.

Pile Sort

The pile sort activity consisted of three header cards and a deck of cards to be sorted. The header cards read: 1) "The church I go to in the free world provides this to former prisoners ALWAYS," 2) "The church I go to in the free world provides this to former prisoners SOMETIMES," and 3) "The church I go to in the free world provides this to former prisoners NEVER." The deck of cards consisted of fifteen cards, each of which had one of the following words printed on it and were stacked, for consistency's sake, alphabetically: Assistance, Dignity, Family, Fellowship, Friends, Hospitality, Love, Nothing, Power, Respect, Safety, Shelter, Support, Voice, and Worship. Subjects were asked to place these cards under whichever header card they felt was most appropriate. Although one weakness of free pile sorts is that it is difficult to compare the data between individuals, I was able to partially overcome this by the use of the header cards and by repeating the exercise three times. Each subject was asked to perform this exercise three times, and each time from a different perspective. The purpose of doing three different versions of this exercise was to determine how well the FIWs are able to anticipate the answers of the PMVs and vice versa. FIWs were asked: (1) How do you believe new converts to Christ in prison would answer this? (2) When you got out of prison, what did you find the churches actually gave you? and, (3) How do you think prison ministry volunteers answer this? Similarly, PMVs were asked: (1) What do you think the church you attend actually provides to former prisoners? (2) How do you believe new converts to Christ in prison would answer this? and, (3) How do you believe women who have left prison would answer this? I intentionally changed the order of the questions between FIWs and PMVs in order to first ask the question from the perspective more personal to the subject, before asking my friends to answer from the other group's perspective.

Chapter 4

What My Friends Teach Us About the Church

As I stated early on, I had come to the conclusion that a discrepancy probably existed between what prison ministry team members meant by church and what women at CIW thought of as church. I therefore shaped a major portion of my interview questions in such a manner as to elicit responses on this topic, to explore the validity of my suppositions. And indeed, my research shows three distinct areas in which rating churches reveals major perception gaps between Formerly Incarcerated Women (FIWs) and Prison Ministry Volunteers (PMVs). These are: (1) how each group rates FIW experiences with PMV church, (2) how each group rates the church at CIW compared to the churches outside prison, and (3) what each subject group believes constitutes a good church.

FIW Experiences with PMV Churches

The first communication gap is revealed in the discrepancies between PMVs' perceptions about FIW experiences with PMV church and the actual FIW description of those experiences. Incredibly, one hundred percent of FIW evaluative responses to attending the churches that had been recommended to them by PMVs were negative; the churches did not meet their expectations. This lies in sharp contrast to the eighty percent of PMVs who reported that FIWs had attended their church, who then rated it a positive experience for those women. This first major finding supports my hypothesis that women in prison are in fact forming expectations of what church is likely to be when they parole, and that their communication with PMVs is not helping them to develop realistic expectations. Having established that the differing experiences of FIWs and PMVs results in the existence of this communication gap then gives meaning and purpose to the rest of my study.

The analysis of PMV responses to this line of inquiry presented some peculiar challenges to me as the researcher. I had personally attended the churches of five of my PMV friends. Surprisingly, only two of those five friends, however, reported that yes, a woman she had ministered to in prison subsequently visited her church. Grace had taken me to her church my first two Sundays after release from CIW in 2010. She said I was okay with it, which was a fair assessment, although I did not experience the vitality of the church at CIW. I did meet several other PMVs there, who were not part of this study but whom I already knew from CIW. But Grace (and the others I met at her church), while having initially participated in CIW church services for a number of years, had ultimately become more of a visitor-cum-mentor, a special category of PMV that I will be discussing in more detail in Chapter 7, regarding mentors.

Of greater challenge and disconnect was the response of three different members of the same church and same CIW prison ministry team, a team that I had worked with inside CIW. Theirs is a megachurch with a campus that comprises two city blocks. I had been invited as a guest speaker to the adult Sunday school class attended by at least one team member, and the entire team had been apprised of my impending engagement and invited to attend. I shared music, testimony, and Scripture with this class. I also guest spoke at an additional Sunday school class in the same building on a different Sunday.

My actual reaction to this mega-church was that I was so overwhelmed by the size and impersonal nature of the campus that it provoked a totally incapacitating panic attack, a form of Post-Traumatic Stress Disorder (PTSD) that I suffer from as a direct result of my thirty-year incarceration. Especially because I was preparing to speak about my prison experience to this adult Sunday school group, I was vulnerable to the triggering of prison memories and reactions. I found myself in a bustling courtyard of people who did not seem to even see me. I was greatly taken aback by the need for and existence of an "Information Booth," but the people at the booth were busy and did not notice me. I was at church, but I was an outsider, a stranger, who could not find my way to where I was supposed to be. In prison, not knowing how to get to where you are supposed to be can have dire consequences, and fear began to well up inside me. I became emotionally paralyzed. My husband, who thankfully was accompanying me, recognized my reaction and pulled me aside. He pointed out a sign that read "Prayer Room" and gently escorted me there. As we attempted to enter the room so that I could pray and be prayed for, a young man explained, "This room is not for the public to pray in. This is the room for the ministry team, where we pray in preparation for giving the church service. The room you want is…" and he gave my husband directions to a distant room that we never found. Instead we returned to our car in the parking lot where I sat and shook and cried. There, an elderly parking lot attendant came to our rescue. The place I was to speak at, he explained, was across the boulevard, in a different building, which had its own parking lot. My husband navigated the traffic and got us to the correct building. I composed myself, put on my gracious guest speaker face, and gave a successful presentation. I was truly happy to see my old friends and meet new friends in this small subset of the larger church. The very characteristics of this mega-church that caused my PTSD attack, however, also meant that none of my PMV friends witnessed or was made aware of my reaction, that of some anonymous woman sobbing and crying while immobilized on a sidewalk in the midst of their church complex.

In an interesting corollary, when I reminded the PMV that I had indeed personally visited her church, Sally explained that although she was cognizant of this before and after my visit, and had heard reports of my speaking to her Sunday school class, because she had not seen me for herself, it did not count. I believe there are two things at play in Sally's response. Her normal experience of church is impersonal, due to its size. She is only aware of the people she actually sees and interacts with at church and does not feel a connection to those who she does not see. Secondly, as I will speak about more in depth in Chapter 7 on Power, because I was a moderator, a leader in the prison church, Sally did not equate me with the psychiatric unit prisoners that we regularly ministered to together. She did not see me as an FIW.

Other FIWs had similar stories. Of particular interest was Diane's observation about her visit to the church of a PMV, and how it compared to her experiences with that same person's ministry inside prison. She explained, "And it was absolutely nothing as I expected it. It was a different theology and a different methodology once I got out here." What makes this observation so important is that the PMV that referred Diane to this church rated the experiences of FIWs who attended there as positive, stating that they were treated "like queens."

In contrast, my PMV friend Bob, who did not rate a different FIW's visit to his church as a positive experience, explained why. "I'm not trying to sound braggadocious or anything, but I think that after they heard me, when they came to the church, they expected the same type of ministry and deliverance, and it was different." Bob recognized that as a PMV he related to women in prison in an entirely different manner than did his pastor to the outside congregation of which Bob was simply a member. Bob's evaluation of the FIW's response to his home church was that he thought she "was kind of disappointed" since she did not have the experience that she was expecting.

CIW Church Compared to Outside Churches

A second discrete communication gap between FIWs and PMVs reveals itself when FIW ratings of how the church at CIW compared to churches outside are analyzed in tandem with PMV ratings of the same church at CIW compared to churches outside. Again, this question was particularly aimed at investigating the validity of my personal perception that there is a major discrepancy between the expectations that paroling women develop regarding church on the outside is based on their experience of the church at CIW—on the inside—and what they subsequently find on the outside. When looking at the category of accepting/loving, which related directly to the two most often mentioned needs of paroling women, although both FIWs and PMVs responses indicate that CIW is positive in this attribute, and while zero responses are given to indicate either CIW as negative for this attribute or the outside church as positive, 70 percent of responses that the outside church is negative for this attribute come from FIWs.

This perceptual gap is even wider for the attributes of real/not superficial. While FIWs (5) and PMVs (4) are in relative agreement that the church at CIW is positive for real/not superficial, only one PMV response rated the outside church as negative on this scale, in contrast to eight negative responses from FIWs. Some FIWs are aware that this discrepancy may not be acknowledged by PMVs. During the pile sort, Tammy noted of the outside church, "I think they always show hospitality, even if it's not real."

Another FIW, Kathy, explained through her tears that, "it's hard to find acceptance." She laments that mega-churches don't seem to care about knowing individuals, and her experience sheds further light on my reaction to the mega-church in the previous section. Specifically, Kathy indicates how this depersonalization impacts her ability to join into their worship:

> Everybody is just off in their own little personal thing and nobody out here really…I haven't found anybody out here, any church out here, that really can corporately worship together and be of one heart and one mind. It's really difficult. Everybody sections off into their own little things, whether it's their own family or their cliques or just being by themselves with one person, you know, with one friend or whatever. It's really strange. I'm not…I don't get it.

PMVs (8) noted much more frequently than FIWs (3) the positive aspect of intensity of worship at CIW, while PMV (2) and FIW (2) equally noted the negative of this in the church outside. I relate this finding to the proverb that one cannot see the forest for the trees, that

FIWs are so immersed in intense worship that such is the norm, and therefore invisible to the insider.

Good Churches Compared to Not Good Churches

The third gap appears when FIW definitions of what differentiates a good church from one that is less good are compared to PMV definitions of what constitutes a good church. Again, FIWs respond more frequently with the good church attribute of being accepting/loving (13) than they do with anything else, even the attribute of teaching the gospel (11). This is in sharp contrast to PMVs who respond with teaching the gospel (23) meaningfully more often than accepting/loving (9).

What this means is that my FIW friends understand a good church to be one that is (listed in order of priority) overwhelmingly accepting, welcoming and non-judgmental, that teaches the gospel, is small and intimate, and provides intense worship opportunities. This is a good description of the church as I knew it for thirty years at CIW. On the other hand, for my PMV friends, a good church is one that overwhelmingly focuses on teaching the gospel, that is accepting, that is small and intimate, and that serves its members.[61] While there is much overlap in these two definitions, these are not the same church! Therefore, this data confirms that one major communication gap between FIWs and PMVs is the difference in their understandings of what the words "good church" means.

One more personal observation gave direction to this study, and caused me to look at expectations. I realized for myself, and later

---

[61] Ironically, as a whole, PMVs define a good church as small and intimate, even when they attend mega-churches.

confirmed with several of my FIW sisters, that upon leaving CIW the only thing I was certain about concerning the churches outside was that I did not know what a "good" church was. The logic goes like this, "If any church I had attended before prison had been a 'good' church, I would never have ended up in prison in the first place." One male African-American PMV subject contested this point. His argument was that most of the women he ministered to at CIW, especially those of his culture, had grown up in the church and knew the church very well. The point he missed is subtle, but vital. There is a difference between being "in" the church and being "of" the church. This was borne out in my interviews with FIWs, many of who admitted to having been raised "in" the church, but who did not identify themselves as saved or committed to Jesus until their incarceration. The church might have thought these women were members, but the women saw themselves as outsiders.[62] One African-American FIW explained the difference, as she described the church at CIW as both where "We worship with all our heart" and that "We did it for us, not grandma."

---

[62] This issue will be discussed further under the "Centered Set Church" discussion.

Factoring out the Nostalgia Factor

I will address here the possibility that the positive ratings by FIWs for the church at CIW could be inaccurate, that FIWs could be viewing the CIW church through rose-colored glasses. Admittedly, the FIWs interviewed for this study are no longer in prison, and some have been away from CIW for ten years or more. However, there are two reasons that make inaccurate ratings due to nostalgia extremely unlikely. First, the original phenomenon that inspired this research (which I discussed in the Introduction of this book) was my observation of women returning to prison and their elation at returning to their "home church" at CIW. Secondly, my personal observation is corroborated by my conversations with FIW friends. During one interview I asked a FIW subject if she had ever noticed the attitudes of the women who, in coming back were not happy to be in prison, but were so very excited to be back in the home church? Ruby replied, "Oh! They missed it!" There was something positive about the church inside prison that was not easily found outside prison.

Secondly, I argue that incarceration is not the sort of experience to be remembered fondly. Prison is a place of dehumanization, shame, pain, and trauma. While the church inside is remembered positively as a gestalt, there were no stained-glass windows bathing the congregation in a rosy glow.

Rating Specific Attributes of Churches

There are ratings of four specific attributes of churches that revealed major perception gaps between FIW and PMV subjects. Specifically, these attributes have to do with how churches live up to providing an atmosphere conducive to experiencing: (1) acceptance and belonging, (2) transformation and new life in Christ, (3) spiritual compared to physical support, and (4) prisoner new convert expectations.

Acceptance and Belonging

It is not that FIWs and PMVs disagree as to whether acceptance from and belonging to a church are important. They do not disagree; both consider providing acceptance and belonging integral to a good church. However, the relative importance each group gives in comparison to other attributes is revealing.

This can most easily be seen by contrasting where each group rates acceptance with where they rate support. Both groups are aware that acceptance and support are important, the gap, the difference, is in degree. The most common first response for FIWs was the need for acceptance while the most common first response for PMVs was the need for support/love. Admittedly, there is some crossover between the two, but it is very difficult for someone who has not experienced the alienation of being convicted of a crime and sent to prison to understand that acceptance might outweigh support/love. Indeed, one of the three PMVs who did rate acceptance first had reported serving a prison sentence in his past. Here is where the GSLC case study of Chapter 9 emphasizes the finding from the interviews in noting that acceptance by the church was stated to be the most important criteria for FIWs.

Due to the acceptance experienced by prisoners attending church at CIW, there is no inhibition in worship. As Diane, an FIW, described it, at church in CIW "you're dealing with a different level of brokenness." What this means is that women in prison react more viscerally when they encounter "anointing on the ministry" of music, song, and worship. Often this reaction includes Pentecostal expressions of worship such as speaking in tongues, being slain in the Spirit, heart wrenching crying and sobbing, exuberant dancing or even laughter in the manner of the Toronto blessing. But what Diane sees as most significant is that "whatever their reaction is to the brokenness that the Holy Spirit is ministering to them, that is what they have the liberty to do."

However, PMV's are not necessarily as accepting of this. Ben's perspective is that prisoners would "disrupt the whole place and say that God is telling them to do that... almost like they're in a trance." Ben proudly explained that his team leader is "pretty bold." He thought it appropriate that he would say, "Now the Holy Spirit is not telling you to do that, so you need to go outside and yell out there."

I will return to this discussion regarding exuberant worship a little further on in this chapter.

Transformation/New Life in Christ

Both PMVs and FIWs remark about the transformation of prisoners as they experience new life in Christ. The gap here is not in perception, but in experience. PMVs acknowledge from the outside that they observe the transformation of prisoners. Ben discusses transformation in terms of hope "for this new life." He observes that prisoners come to believe in God as their Lord and Savior, and that they have peace. But Ben is "not comfortable" admitting "I'm going to say they have joy even, in spite of the fact that they're in prison." He then explains that "they seem to be more appreciative" of God's working in their lives "because of their lack of hope of anything."

Another PMV, Lisa, addresses how different this experience is from the general experience of people in the churches outside:

> When I watch the women, and when I'm part of it, I feel like they've experienced transformation in a way that people who have gone to church for most of their lives don't get. There's something that comes from their spirit... and they've tasted of that in a way that people who've been life-long Christians haven't been.

From the FIW side, the inside, Ruby explains the transformation she experienced in prison as finding Jesus "in the destitute, in the darkness, when there's nothing to distract you." When all previous coping mechanisms and everything a prisoner was accustomed to has been taken away, "It's just you and Him. You come face to face with Him. So that's what it is about the Christian faith inside those walls."

So while Ruby does agree with Ben that believing in Jesus gives hope, she also conveys how the dominant language leaves her with insufficient words to describe this experience.

> It gives you hope. Um…I don't think the English words, or no words, have the proper definition to give to you concerning it. All I can use is our mediocre words, is that it gives you a hope that's, ah…that supersedes anything.

Another FIW, Rosa, in broken English, describes her experience of transformation:

> I start to know the word of God, I st…I knew that there is a God exist, and He has control of my life. He is the one to do the miracles in my life every day. The…that moments that I have to understand who is God and…and how I can depend on Him even though…um…in the worst place.

And finally, Kathy explains that transformation is the common experience of women who come to Christ in prison. Further, this experience is what constitutes their testimonies. When asked if she experienced a difference between churches inside and outside prison, Kathy got so excited, "Oh my gosh!!! So much!! The hugest!! Hugest difference. Oh my gosh! In prison, there are no pretenses. We are who we are." What she is referring to is that it is impossible to hide from our unsavory pasts in prison, so we "openly admit to the things that we were a part of. And…that's part of our testimony."

While such transformations do occur outside prison, they are usually not as dramatic nor as universal a characteristic; it is not the shared experience of everyone in the churches outside. However, in the church at CIW, this level of transformation is the majority experience.

Spiritual Compared to Physical Support

A second gap revealed in Q#2, Important for Churches to Offer Paroling Women, has to do with the relative importance of spiritual versus physical support. The results of my research were completely contrary to what would be expected from the literature.[63] What I looked at here was not only what was said in the verbal responses to the question, but the placement (whether this was the first, second, third, etc., item given in an oral list. Less than a third, only 30 percent, of FIW responses had to do with the importance of physical support, and only one of those was a first response. However, not only did 40 percent of PMV responses referred to physical support, but seven of those were first responses. One reason given by Eva for the FIW priority to spiritual/emotional needs is that "the other...we can easily find." Eva was referring to the presence of food pantries, homeless shelters, and other basic need resources that Parole Officers and re-entry programs provide or direct former prisoners to. However, spiritual support is particularly important because, she further clarified, "if you're not rooted and grounded, you're not going to make it."

How this ultimately plays out is that while five PMVs listed food, and two of those as first response, not a single FIW named food as something that is important for churches to offer paroling women. One PMV, Grace, specifically named "taking them out to meals" as part of

---

[63] Nicole M. Morani, Nora Wikoff, Donald M. Linhorst and Sheila Bratton, "A Description of the Self-Identified Needs, Service Expenditures, and Social Outcomes of Participants of a Prisoner-Reentry Program." *The Prison Journal* 91 (3) (2011): 348.

what she called the "help in the adjustment" that churches should be providing. Judy, a PMV, said about the women she ministered to upon release from prison that, "they liked especially the brunch; the women's brunch. It was a meal thing." From Judy's perspective, for the recently paroled it was a "new thing to do."

This attitude of PMVs towards feeding FIWs is borne out by my observation that of all of the PMVs who chose to be interviewed at restaurants, the only two who did not insist on paying for my order were the two who had self-identified as themselves having, in the past, served time in prison.

Julie's response to being taken out for a meal was, "Oh my God! It was like, everybody want [sic] to buy you food. You know, take you somewhere to eat, but nobody want to really help you with the things you really need." For that matter, being taken out for meals was an almost daily event my first week out of prison. And the first stop my parole agent made after picking me up at CIW was In and Out Burgers, presuming it was going to be a great treat for me to spend part of my $200 "gate money" for fast food. I was appalled, but politely thanked him and bought the most inexpensive thing I could find on the menu. Given the power dynamic that my continuing freedom depended upon the good graces of my parole agent, I was muted.

In the last seven years I have come to understand that in dominant culture outside prison, taking someone out for a meal is what one does for a friend. However, I am also aware that this is not the prison experience. At CIW, leaving the housing unit and going to where the food is served, to the Culinary, is what one does with total strangers. If you are my friend, I invite you to my cell, my haven, and prepare a meal for you from my scarce resources. PMVs are eager to feed FIW bodies as part of ministry, but only on neutral ground; not by accepting them into their home. A gap exists between this and the FIW perspective that, while they can look to anyone to provide food for the body, they look to PMVs to feed their spirits and souls with the gospel of Christ.

One more gap revealed here relates to the topic of reintegration assistance, which eleven PMVs but only one FIW identified as important for churches to offer paroling women. Even though pile sort data says that fifty-three percent of FIWs believe that New Converts (NCs) expect churches to provide shelter always compared to twenty-one percent of PMVs, this expectation does not translate into what FIWs believe is most important. Just because FIWs have an expectation does not necessarily mean the thing expected is considered all that important. Possible explanations for this apparent contradiction include the FIW's experiences of physical assistance being channeled through the Parole Office, and the perceived naïvety of NCs in reflection. Nevertheless, the difference between PMV and FIW perceptions of the relative importance of physical and spiritual needs of paroling women is meaningful.

Prisoner New Convert (NC) Expectations

The pile sort activity was specifically designed to investigate newly converted prisoners' expectations of the church outside, and how well the PMVs understand the NCs expectations. Perhaps FIWs perception of NC expectations are somewhat colored by the idealism of memory. However, given that each of them, by qualifying for this study, had at one time been that NC, their answers are the measuring rod used here. To be consistent with how this data is presented elsewhere in this book, elements such as worship are written in *italics*, while the headings of **always, sometimes,** and **never** are written in bold.

Several distinct findings emerge from the pile sort that, when synthesized, paint a clear picture of the communication gap dynamic regarding prisoner converts' expectations of the churches outside. First, compared to PMVs, FIWs rated the NCs as more optimistic, of expecting more from the churches on the outside when they paroled, with more than fifty percent of FIWs rating **always** on each and every element. PMVs are more moderate in their evaluations, thinking NCs believe the churches offer them these elements **sometimes** and only *worship* being an exception at seventy-nine percent **always**.

Second, FIWs think that PMVs believe their churches give these elements to paroling women **always**. This belief is so strong that three different FIW subjects, instead of rating each element card individually, slapped the entire deck down on **always**. Ruby did so with such vehemence that she shocked herself. The follow excerpt from the interview transcription makes this clear. I had asked how the PMVs were answering the question "The church I go to in the free world provides this to former prisoners…" and before I could read the options:

Me. (loud bang) (laughs). YES! Slammed that whole package on top of **always**…
Ruby. Because that's what they believe.
Me. Thank you. Um…
Ruby. That's what I feel they believe.
Me. That's what I'm asking for.
Ruby. Wow. Boy did I go that deep? I was like, Wow! (both laugh) I didn't even think about that. That was weird. That didn't come from me, Linda. That was straight from the Holy Spirit, because…I…I…I wouldn't have got that idea on my own. Okay? Cause I was shocked when I did it. I was like, Wow.

However, these strong beliefs of the FIWs about the PMVs are not borne out by the evidence. In fact, of the three PMVs who slapped an entire deck of cards that listed individual resources down while doing the pile sort activity, two of them said their churches provide the entire deck to paroling women **sometimes**, while a third said **never**.

Interestingly, what this means is that PMVs actually have realistic expectations of what their churches are offering paroling women, yet incorrectly believe they are communicating this to NCs inside CIW. The FIWs are saying that realistic expectations are not being communicated to new converts inside CIW, and that therefore the NCs have unrealistic expectations of the outside churches. And these unrealistic expectations impact the NCs when they are ultimately confronted with reality upon parole. The dynamics of this communication gap will be further discussed in Chapter 6 under the topic of "Honesty."

What are the hidden values of the CIW church model? What do these findings then tell us about the churches inside and outside prison that we were not previously aware of? And how can this data inform the church in its practice of mission? The major missiological implication of this research that will be discussed next involve what it means that CIW is a centered-set church.

A Different Side to Church-dom

Diane made a poignant comment that describes a feeling that most of my FIW friends had trouble expressing. What she said was, "I think we all have learned that there is a different side to church-dom out here." By "we" she is referring to us FIWs, those of us who have experienced both the church at CIW and the church outside. And by the "different side," she is expressing the loss of an intimate, exuberant, community of believers where there is an amazing freedom in expressing one's faith in Jesus Christ. However, the PMVs who notice this difference do not always see CIW in a positive light.

It is really mind blowing to most people outside to realize how many worship opportunities there are in prison. Church services are not limited to Sunday mornings and Wednesday evenings. This schedule results in prisoners being able to attend services and studies every single day. It also means that each prisoner is attending services and studies that are led by various denominations. The PMVs who lead these may hold to vastly differing doctrines.

One PMV, Sally, explained at length how, from her perspective, the CIW church structure differs from the church outside and thus affects both the ability of a ministry team to give consistent teaching to the prisoners, and the ability of prisoners to develop a cohesive theology. She pointed out the number of different churches and ministry groups that are regularly scheduled by the Protestant Chaplain (see Appendix B, Protestant Service Schedule, November 2016). She then contrasted this with regular attendance at an outside church where "when you're in a church for a while...you really get a chance to sort of establish a baseline." Inside CIW, she notes, prisoners are often attending several different ministries and Bible studies during the week, some of which are just among themselves, therefore, "...it's like everybody establishes their own baseline." She perceives this as a problem because the women are receiving teachings in capsules of twenty to thirty minutes, without receiving real guidance as to how to synthesize all the different teachings. This results, Sally says, in them "trying to put things together like a puzzle, if you will, and the pieces don't fit."

Another PMV, Ben, explains the ramifications of the lack of obvious structure as resulting in the prisoners developing "misguided beliefs." Ben expressed admiration of a fellow PMV team member who was "pretty bold," and would quiet prisoners who were too loud in worship by saying, "the Holy Spirit is not telling you to do that so you need to go outside and yell out there." He also voiced frustration that the Chaplain's response to the above would most likely be "No, that was the anointing of the Holy Spirit." FIWs such as Diane agreed that this would be the Chaplain's response, but voiced gratitude rather than frustration, referring to it as having the "liberty" to worship as the "anointing" leads at CIW.

An additional aspect of the church in CIW that differs from churches outside is that new converts in prison are all recipients of evangelism or mission outreach to prisoners, so they do not identify evangelistic outreach as something "special" but instead it is part of this prison church norm. Ben has a different perspective and experience. His understanding of the church outside is that:

> But very few churches go out into the world and preach the gospel. That's the biggest missing link. And this is an area, just to go back on the other question, where the church on the inside generally did a better job. They were not ashamed of their faith for the most part, and they let it be known.

I find this much of his understanding to be accurate. However, since his experience at CIW only reflected the study that he personally led, his further reflection is less accurate.

> I actually taught an evangelism class at CIW and the women were awesome. It kinda got cut short, but we got two out of the three classes in. So, they were out there on

the yard, and I think for the first time in the history of CIW, preaching the gospel to people walking by. I don't think that's ever been done.

In fact, however, evangelism on the yard is a commonplace activity. It is simply not rare enough to merit comment by FIWs, who assume that this is simply part of how any good church functions. I was reminded by my FIW friend Diane that I had personally conducted a weekly evangelistic singing event out in the middle of the yard every Saturday evening for almost a decade. "When you talk about prisoners talking about prison ministry...they're talking about it from a view of what they have experienced...firsthand. I still can remember women talking about your circles. 'And what was her name? She played the guitar.'"

At least one FIW subject of this study had been a leader in PATCH (Preaching And Teaching Christ Here), a prisoner-initiated-and -led group that was teaching and evangelizing on the main yard[64] with the Chaplain only providing the smallest amount of supervision necessary to make it a legally recognized prison group. As will be discussed in Chapter 9, the Good Shepherd Lutheran Church case study, member-initiated interest groups are extremely effective at mobilizing a church. PATCH at CIW was no exception. What made PATCH noteworthy is that the Chaplain deliberately empowered prisoners to take leadership roles without relying on PMVs for supervision and guidance.

The same thing occurs with the idea of a church serving its members. But for prisoners who convert to Christ in prison, what is new

---

[64] Prison idiom is "on the yard" and never "in the yard."

is the experience of being accepted and of belonging.[65]. Many or most PMVs, on the other hand, have always experienced the church as accepting and as something to which they have perhaps belonged since birth, and therefore do not perceive this as special.

---

[65] This relates to why I refrain from using the "re" words, like rehabilitation, reentry, and reintegration. By definition, persons from subdominant groups have never entered or integrated with the dominant culture in the first place.

Chapter 5

California Institution for Women:

A Centered Set Church

The church at the California Institution for Women (CIW) is a church without walls, within walls. This chapter will explore the intersection between the unique structure of the CIW church, Hiebert's centered set theory of boundaries and membership, and Muted Group Theory (MGT). Unexpected, and missionally fruitful, interfaith friendships are formed as a result of this intersection, with implications of great value to urban mission and churches outside prison.

I therefore begin this chapter with an introductory overview of Hiebert's theory regarding bounded set/centered set church dynamics. After laying this groundwork, I describe the factors that contribute to CIW evolving into a centered set church. Then I explain the relationship between CIW as a centered set church and the interfaith friendships that develop at CIW. Finally, I discuss the implications of the CIW model as it relates to urban mission. Throughout I will intersperse stories about my CIW friends, experiences that illustrate the prison context of a centered set church, and how all of this is related to MGT power dynamics.

Hiebert and Set Theory

Paul Hiebert first used the mathematical set model to describe how the church determines who is Christian in terms of bounded set/centered set in his 1978 article, "How much must Papayya 'know' about the Gospel to be Converted?"[66] His treatment of set theory as applied to the category Christian and to the task of Christian mission continues to be influential and to merit reflection by missiologists.[67] I had first been introduced to Hiebert's work while I was still incarcerated and doing master's degree theology work by distance learning. I felt an immediate affinity to this concept, but really did not realize its significance to the church at CIW as I was experiencing it at the time. Hiebert identifies and describes three different types of sets.

Bounded Sets

In set theory, bounded sets are all about static boundaries, and whoever is within the criteria for membership. It requires immediate change in all essential characteristics for a non-member to become a member of a bounded set.[68] Thus, the static boundaries of a bounded set church may include such membership criteria as a salvation event, baptism, adherence to creeds, and conformity to community norms.

---

[66] Paul G. Hiebert, "How much must Papayya 'know' about the Gospel to be Converted?" *Gospel in Context* 1 (4), (1978): 24-29.

[67] Michael L. Yoder, Michael H. Lee, Jonathan Ro and Robert J. Priest, "Understand Christian Identity in Terms of Bounded and Centered Set Theory in the Writings of Paul G. Hiebert." *Trinity Journal* 30 (2)(2009): 187.

[68] Yoder et al, "Understand Christian Identity," 180.

Bounded set thinking can lead to "closed mindedness" since this model emphasizes the "otherness" of outsiders. Most churches are thus bounded sets, each with a roster of members who conform to the criteria set for membership.

Centered Sets

Centered sets, however, are dynamic. Instead of defining a boundary, what is defined in a centered set is the center, and relationship to the center. Although they may vary in distance from it, members are moving towards, or are in relationship to, the center. Thus change, in centered set perspective, involves entry into or out of the set, or movement to or from the center.[69] Hiebert explains that while centered sets do have well-formed boundaries, greater emphasis is placed on the center and relationships than on maintaining a boundary for the reason that there is no need to maintain the boundary in order to maintain the set.[70] In the centered set church, the center is Christ Jesus, therefore, those who are true disciples but differ in race, class, gender, or theological viewpoint are equally valued members of the set.[71]

Fuzzy Sets

A final distinction, according to Hiebert, exists between well-bounded sets and fuzzy sets. Fuzzy sets do not have distinct boundaries. In fuzzy sets, change is a process, not a point or turnaround, and is based on continuum instead of sharp transition. However, the

---

[69] Ibid.

[70] Paul G. Hiebert, *Anthropological Reflections on Missiological Issues*, Grand Rapids, MI: Baker Books, 1994, 124.

[71] Ibid., 128.

distinctions between bounded sets and fuzzy sets, while significant in themselves, are not the focus in the limited space of this work.[72]

CIW as a Centered Set Church

I have come to realize that CIW is a centered set church. There is no formal membership to the CIW church; if you are moving towards Jesus, then you are part of the church. Baptism at CIW is not about becoming part of a specific denomination nor has it any organizational consequence. Instead, repentance, which results in turning away from sin and towards Christ is enough for membership, even if behavior is not yet fully conformed to the ideal.

The church within prison walls is a church without walls. What I mean by this is that the prison wall is a far more determinative boundary to prisoners than any church wall. Even though prison walls, in physical aspects might be impermeable, the prison church walls are much more permeable than the walls of churches outside. Church activity inside prison is open to public view. In the church without walls at CIW, everyone gets to watch Christians being Christians in a way that is not usually duplicated elsewhere. What is generally experienced as enclosed "safe place" worship, at CIW is something that occurs in public.

Evolution of CIW into a Centered Set Church

The church at CIW is unique in many distinct ways, three of which are of particular interest in the discussion of CIW as a centered set

---

[72] Roger E. Olson, *Reformed and Always Reforming: The Postconservative Approach to Evangelical Theology*, Grand Rapids, MI: Baker Academic, 2007, 59 fn45. I lean towards Olson's position, that it is possible, and perhaps necessary, that the church is a fuzzy/centered set. They are like fuzzy sets in that they "have no sharp, definable boundaries to any human intelligence," but "differ from fuzzy sets in having a strong center."

church. Specifically, I will be looking at: (1) the physical layout of the church at CIW, (2) how the leadership functions, and (3) the status of the church members. Each of these factors contributes to how and why CIW has evolved into a centered-set church.

Physical Layout of the CIW Church

First and most obvious of these factors is the physical layout of the church at CIW. CIW is a prison built in Southern California and opened in 1953. CIW is a prison surrounded by chain link fence and razor wire. Only staff and outside prison ministry volunteers (PMVs) are free to leave the local area when church services are over. Space is at a premium at CIW. Housing units that were built with single occupancy cells are now all double occupancy, with a total population of around two thousand women. The Protestant church does not have its own chapel, but instead shares a larger Interfaith Chapel. PMVs often remark about the difficulties they experience due to their being no separate Protestant Church building in CIW. One perceived difficulty is that many church services and Bible studies must, out of necessity, be held in areas other than the chapel. This means that alternative spaces such as education classrooms, drug program classrooms, and for large events, the institution auditorium, also serve as sacred space. The Interfaith Chapel itself consists of a doublewide modular unit and offers a sanctuary area surrounded by offices. Thus, the Interfaith Chapel is shared sacred space. Protestant, Catholic, Jewish, and Muslim services and events all occur in this sanctuary area, resulting in a church without normal physical boundaries.

Out on the Circle: The grassy central area around which all the housing units are arranged at CIW is referred to as "the circle." Given that there are not enough available rooms for all the faith related activities, many informal activities occur "out on the circle." What is meaningful about this is that, yet again, faith activities are occurring in a church without physical walls.

For almost a decade, during a period of time when there were no official Protestant church activities occurring on Saturday evenings, I took my guitar and a folder of song sheets "out on the circle." A group of women would form around me as I led in singing praise songs. Small groups of women sitting at a distance would edge closer, and often enter in. No one ever asked them, "Are you one of us?"

It was not just me. As I mentioned earlier, a prisoner led discipleship group, PATCH (Preaching And Teaching Christ Here) met "out on the circle" on weekend afternoons. The prisoner leaders of this group actively discipled new Christians. They also led interactive Bible studies. And the group as a whole did active evangelizing, handing out tracts to whoever was walking by.

My cellmate for the final thirteen years of my incarceration, an indigenous Mixtec from Mexico, led Spanish speaker Bible studies several nights a week, rain or shine, "out on the circle." The high visibility of these ministry events means that everyone who passed by was aware of who was leading, who was participating, and who was peripheral to all of these activities.

How Leadership Functions at the Interfaith Chapel

Counter-intuitively, Chaplains do not have the time resources to personally conduct more than a minimal number of services and events. Instead, the primary work of staff chaplains is to facilitate the bureaucratic paperwork necessary in order for PMVs to enter the institution and conduct activities, and to provide oversight of these PMVs and their programs. The other main duties of staff chaplains, duties that cannot be delegated to PMVs, are delivering death notices when a prisoner's family member dies, providing emergency pastoral counseling to prisoners and staff, and supervising "inmate workers." Each and every service or event necessitates a chain of signed written approvals and clearances. If the paperwork that states a person or team is cleared to enter the institution is missing, that service or event will be cancelled. Often, multiple approvals are needed for a single event; one for volunteers to enter the institution, another for food to be brought into the prison, another reserving a specific room, and yet another that allows prisoners to be excused from their jobs to attend the event. Therefore, since all the Chaplains are institutional staff, if the Protestant Chaplain is not available to sign paperwork or find missing paperwork or facilitate an event, prisoners are just as likely to go to the Catholic Chaplain, Rabbi, or Imam for assistance. The same applies to prisoners' personal emergencies; they are likely to call upon whichever chaplain is in the institution.

There is another aspect of prison chaplaincy that contributes to the centered set perspective and promotion of interfaith friendships; respect for other faiths is mandated by the State of California. The CIW Protestant Chaplain explained to me during her interview for my research that she specifically trains volunteers to not proselytize or in any way put down another denomination or faith, "In other words, we do not...go against another religion there at the prison." So what will be discussed as a drawback and communication gap later on in Chapter 6, that PMVs are trained to not discuss denominations, is a positive contributing factor to the centered set church.

The United States constitutional separation of church and state is expressed differently in prison than in the culture at large. At CIW it means that, on one hand, staff are not allowed to proselytize, and even the chaplains must, by law, be respectful of all faiths. These boundaries are clear and inflexible for the PMVs. On the other hand, prisoners cannot be prevented from expressing their faith or attending faith-based activities. If staff are concerned that attendance at an event might result in an unmanageable situation, such as might occur at a special banquet, membership can only be determined by who has attended that particular group for a particular length of time. So for prisoners, the boundaries that might limit membership are, in effect, unenforceable.

Dealing with Officer Mendez

The public nature of worship at CIW, and staff being legally unable to abolish or hinder worship, has interesting repercussions. Officer Mendez was particularly hostile to Christian prisoners. When I would be leading Bible study in my housing unit day room, she would make a point of standing directly behind me and shouting orders to someone at a distance, simply in order to deliberately disrupt us. She would make devil's horns behind my head with her fingers. She would try anything to irritate me, and the circle of women around me. Our response was to pray. Within her hearing, we would pray all of God's blessings on her. Eventually, in the normal sequence of staff rotations, this officer was reassigned to the adjacent housing unit. A few months later, a Christian prisoner from that unit actually led this officer to Christ. Within weeks, my new sister in Christ, Officer Mendez, sent for me. She asked me if I could hold a Bible study in her unit.

This underlying dynamic of the CIW centered set church is omnipresent. Worship is a public event, how one lives one's Christian life is visible to outsiders, and this openness often leads to respect, relationship, and ultimately friendship. Powerless and muted prisoners are able to express themselves through presence, through being seen even if they are not initially heard. And sometimes this results in the powerful acting to deliberately provide voice to the powerless.

Status of Church Members

By status of the members, I am referring to the fact that CIW is a prison and the congregation is comprised of prisoners. Although obvious, it is significant to note that no one moves into this community simply due to a desire to find a community of fellow believers! And although there are choices available as to which particular service, study, or fellowship to attend or not attend, prisoners do not have the choice to relocate to a different community. This forced aspect of the permanence and transiency of the members is also unusual. Prisoners serving life sentences cannot relocate, while prisoners serving short-term sentences are forced to leave the CIW church when they parole.

There is no formal membership to the CIW church. Christians are those who, as my FIW friend Eva so eloquently describes it, "are on their way to Jesus." In other words, any prisoner who is "on her way to Jesus," is considered part of the church. Another aspect of the CIW church that is distinct from most churches outside is that since it is not a church you can be born into and raised within, everyone has experienced a personal "entering" into the set, which in itself makes for a perception of more permeable boundaries. Almost every Christian prisoner's personal history includes a turning point. Few, indeed, are the prisoners who assert that they have never turned away from Jesus. And those few who do so are generally held suspect.

Something I would not have expected except that my husband pointed it out to me, is that it may surprise some people to hear that the presence of outsiders does not necessarily dilute the intense worship experience of women in prison. There is a universal understanding among prisoners who convert to Christ in or immediately before prison that they, too, were initially outsiders who, as we referred to them above, were "on their way to meet Jesus." What it really boils down to is that, whether women in prison are thinking that there are no outsiders, or that everyone is an outsider, we are all on the same side of the prison wall. Such is the shared experience of the subdominant prisoners.

The Centered Set Church Promotes Interfaith Friendships

At CIW there is a unique interdependence between the faith communities. People simply must work together to get things done in an environment where it is always difficult to get things done. Prisoners are at the bottom of the power hierarchy in prison. Thus, rather than relying on personal ability or power structures, using MGT language, subdominant muted prisoners learn to rely on cooperative relationships and mutual benefit.

Cooperative relationships take unexpected forms in prison. The need for bureaucratic oversight of unpaid PMVs results in strange bedfellows for the paid staff Chaplains. The Protestant Chaplain oversees Jehovah Witness and Mormon volunteers and programs. The Rabbi oversees the Wicca volunteers and programs. The Catholic Chaplain oversees the Native American volunteers and programs.

My FIW friend Diane gave one example of how this interfaith cooperation works. She put it in terms of taking pressure off the Chaplains. "It didn't matter which Chaplain it was" that was overburdened at the moment, prisoners "just approached whichever Chaplain was able to step in to take part of the workload" of processing paperwork or facilitating events.

Eva the Clerk

Eva was "totally sold out to Jesus" but still worked for years as the Rabbi's inmate clerk. Additionally, she was very active in the Shalom Sisterhood, the prison's Jewish self-help group, even serving as vice-chairperson for some years. Membership in such groups is not a bounded set for a variety of reasons. As previously stated, State law prohibits the exclusion of anyone from attending a religious activity of their choosing for any reason except that of institutional security. An additional and utterly pragmatic reason for many non-Jewish prisoners to join the Shalom Sisterhood besides faith is that they were renown for holding great feasts, catered by outside Jewish PMVs, for such holidays as Passover. Leftovers from these feasts were commodities not to be scorned. Passover matzo makes a great communion wafer, practically and theologically. Simultaneous to being the Rabbi's clerk, Eva held a position as elder in the Protestant church. Ultimately, when that Rabbi retired and was replaced, Eva changed jobs and became the Protestant Chaplain's clerk.

In addition to the Interfaith Chapel not serving to physically contain the CIW church, this shared space results in a permeable boundary between faiths. At CIW, this results in a church lacking those boundaries that outside churches think of as normal. Not only does the building not contain the church, outsiders are often present in the proximal area, even and especially during worship events. The reality is that there are many reasons that women in prison might choose to attend a church service besides the desire to worship. Some come in for air-conditioning, others as a meeting place to see friends, and yet others as simply a place to be that exists outside the confinement of their cells. But it is just as likely that the women sitting in the back row of the Interfaith Chapel during a Protestant service may well be waiting to speak to the Rabbi, or to have Muslim prayer upon completion of the Protestant service, or to discuss the next Native American event with the Catholic Chaplain.

I have come to realize that another perceptual gap that has caused me consternation is explained by the idea that CIW is a centered set church. I have frequently been amazed to hear from PMVs inside prison, and from Christians outside prison, that they do not know any non-Christians. This sharing of space that is not understood by PMVs, and which some refer to as a negative aspect of the church at CIW, however, means that Christian prisoners are constantly living a witness to non-Christians. The common life experience of Christian prisoners is that we work, live, and even worship shoulder to shoulder with our sisters of other faiths.

Centered Set Church Leads to Unusual Friendships

I was privileged to have institutional clearance to provide Protestant services to CIW's psychiatric unit. What this entailed was being granted special security clearance to a controlled access section of the prison. Since the Jehovah Witness PMV simultaneously held a service in a separate room in the same psychiatric unit, we found it expedient to coordinate our efforts so that we walked together across the main yard, through the main sally port, the secondary gates, and finally into the unit together. We could hardly do so without becoming cordial. Eventually, we became friends enough to even be able to compare our differing theologies.

Bounded set churches have a severely limited definition of who is defined as close. This can result in an insulated enclave of like believers. At CIW one is an insider by virtue of her institutional number, whether she has resided there for three hours or three decades, and no matter what her personal beliefs. All CIW prisoners are neighbors.

Millie and Sparrow: Another example of interfaith friendship comes from my own story. I was working as a tutor/facilitator for a community college program within the prison. Millie was a fellow tutor, and Sparrow was a student. Since the entire college program was assigned to dine together, these two became my regular dinner partners, sharing the same table with me. What made this relationship unusual is that Millie was a Wicca priestess and Sparrow a Wicca member, and yet everyone knew that I identified with the Protestant church. Millie was Hawaiian, Sparrow was Native American, and both were seeking for a faith that acknowledged and empowered them as women, and had settled on Wicca and goddess worship. There were some in the church who criticized the closeness of my friendship with these women. And yet, while I do not know exactly why they made the request of me, these two women asked me to teach them how to play "Amazing Grace" on guitar. I also don't know what they did with it, but while I was teaching them, they were exposed to the presence of the Holy Spirit as well as the words of this iconic hymn.

Due to power differences that are inherent in a prison, the strange reality is that the distance between a Christian prisoner and the Protestant Chaplain is often much greater than the distance between that same prisoner and sisters of other faiths. After all, these fellow prisoners are also co-workers, close neighbors, and even cellmates. Thus, the term neighbor is more meaningful in a community of two thousand women than it may be for most people in the dominant free culture. In prison "bed moves" are made at the convenience of the institution; on any day, at any time, such institutional convenience may mean that a prisoner's new cellmate is that Muslim woman she saw at the chapel yesterday. Staying on moderately good terms with everyone is vital in a closed environment where you do not know who will be assigned to work next to you. Unlike men's institutions, which tend to be both larger and more impersonal and where racial and social segregation is the norm, at CIW the women generally coexist peacefully. Arguments and fights are usually personal matters and the level of violence is generally not life threatening.

This also means that a prisoner's lifestyle witness to nonbelievers is much stronger at CIW than is often the case elsewhere. There are very few secrets in prison. Cement walls carry the sounds of arguing voices as clearly as paper-thin walls in other environments. A believer cannot so easily act one way in church and another way in her personal life when under 24-hour-a-day observation.

Implications of the Centered Set Church Model

I am not suggesting that churches should suddenly discard their membership policies and tear down their physical walls. However, what might be the result if we were willing to take a lesson from CIW and start looking at outsiders from more of a centered set perspective? CIW interfaith friendships are not limited to prison, but actually transcend the prison walls. I correspond with some of the friends I left behind in prison. Recently, my husband brought in the mail and handed me three letters from CIW. One is from a friend who is active in the Catholic community at CIW. The second friend is the Rabbi's clerk. The third friend is a leader in the Muslim sisterhood.

Maybe the CIW centered set model cannot be directly transplanted into our community churches. However, the relationships that formed at CIW that span beyond the walls when someone leaves the prison can eventually be brought out to the community intact. I have been introducing my friends to my small ELCA church, explaining the background of each as well as the depth of my relationships. These are not just my friends; we have become sisters. And now my church family outside is supporting my prisoner family inside as they face the parole board, even when they are from other faiths (i.e. Muslim). The support letters written by church members are specific about this, although these women are welcome to visit or join us, support for their parole is not contingent upon their professing Protestant Christian faith.

There is another way interfaith friendship is being promoted by the relationships between prisoners and the church outside, but which has been partially placed on hold for the moment due to the heartbreaking realities of interfaith relationships in our society at large. My Lutheran pastor, as a leader in the local interfaith council, joined me in offering to approach the local leaders of the mosque in order to gain more support for my Muslim friend who is facing the parole board soon. However, my friend regretfully declined our offer: "Please do not contact the mosque." She is afraid for the parole board to associate her with Islam, as this would make her appear to be more of a threat to society. So she welcomes the support letters from the Protestant church, but requests that we only approach the mosque if she is actually granted parole. This is not a prisoner's paranoia; this is simply a Muslim woman's reality, and a forceful argument for the need to foster more interfaith friendships within our culture. Interfaith friendships can break through isolating boundaries and provide opportunities for showing love and human concern in Christ's name.

This is in sharp contrast to someone I know who, when meeting anyone new, puts words into her speech that are "tests" to see if someone is already Christian. If they are, all is well and good. If they are not, then she lies in wait for a chance to throw "Jesus bombs" at them. This is not a very productive manner to conduct interfaith friendship. Instead, interfaith friendships call for a special kind of humility. It is a humility that realizes that no one knows if or when someone else might be starting to look towards Jesus and therefore might be moving towards inclusion in the centered set church. Rather than working to determine whether persons meet membership criteria, it is much more loving and efficacious to support those persons on their journey towards Jesus.

There are two types of walls: the visible concrete (pun intended) walls and those walls that are invisible but just as insurmountable. These latter walls are sometimes even stronger and more effective at keeping out the "other." What might happen if churches were to lower some of the visible and invisible walls? What would this look like? Here is another example from CIW.

Potlucks

One additional activity that was often held "out on the circle" was potluck meals. Here membership was slightly more bounded, but I emphasize, only slightly. While prisoners have hundreds of different recipes for what can be made with ramen noodles, many women at CIW cannot afford even the twenty-five cents that one package of ramen costs. It was a quite common occurrence at potlucks for somebody to sidle up and identify herself as a "friend of a friend" in hopes of being asked to join the meal. More often than not, she would be treated as an insider and given food. How many churches are unwilling to hold their annual church picnic in an area that would attract transient, homeless, or otherwise non-members to join? How many would think to invite a mosque or temple to co-host such an event?

Another way to think "out of the box" is to contemplate the possibility that not all church worship and worship-related events have to be located behind the sanctuary doors. The church can be more intentional about holding visible open events such as picnics, music concerts, and community service events. Special worship services, such as outdoor Easter vigils or Christmas posadas can be held where they are visible. On the opposite end of the spectrum, church members can be more deliberate about accepting invitations from non-Christians to interfaith celebrations. This is not watering down the Christian faith, but simply knowing that Jesus is the center, and that he has the power to transform people while they are journeying towards him.

Familiarity

Many Saturday mornings in prison I woke to the jingling sound of the Native American Chaplain, in full Lakota Sioux regalia, walking past my window on his way to the sweat lodge. The wafting scent of sage, burnt to purify the grounds, and the regular pounding of Indian drums carried to my cell. Many of my friends, whether or not they were First Nations people, regularly attended the sweats. Many of them considered themselves Christians. Again, in an environment of scarce resources, leftovers provided a welcome commodity. For many years, I seasoned my makeshift prison Thanksgiving Dinner bread stuffing with sage that had been given to me by my Native American sisters.

This familiarity with those who practice traditional Native American ways means that I am comfortable visiting the annual Powwow held a mile from my current home, mingling with my neighbors and becoming friends. In other words, living in a Centered Set church environment creates more possibilities for shared life experiences and therefore decreases the chances of unintentional muting. The way to create a more Centered Set church environment is to open our eyes to the presence of Christ, and to the work of the Holy Spirit, in the lives of those we consider outsiders. This will allow us to see Christ in others and to demonstrate the love of Christ in our relationships with others.

My Friend Marge

I would like to introduce you to my best friend and closest ministry partner, Marge. It was a tragic loss for all of us when she died as the result of poor medical care after an elective surgery, while still incarcerated at CIW. The institution's reaction to her passing was not only a tribute to her Christian witness; it provides a perfect example of how the centered set church of which she was such a pillar promotes interfaith friendships. Marge had worked for many years in the prison Inmate Appeals Office, and had a reputation of fairness, kindness, and (rare in the prison bureaucracy) efficiency with paperwork, that was part of the interdependence of life at CIW. So many people wanted to attend Marge's memorial service that it was necessary to hold it in the auditorium; the Interfaith Chapel was not large enough. It sounds like the opening of a classic joke, "The priest, the rabbi, and the minister all show up at a funeral." But the truth is that all the faith communities at CIW acknowledged Marge as a woman of faith. Marge had been raised a nominal Catholic, and was on cordial terms with the Catholic priest. However, while in county jail prior to her arrival at CIW Marge had found a deeper relationship with Jesus in the Protestant faith, and was considered an elder in the CIW Protestant community. Marge also regularly attended the Rabbi's Judaism classes, in order to broaden her own understanding of the Old Testament heritage. Thus everyone, staff and prisoner alike, found it appropriate that all the chaplains shared in presiding over her service. It is important to note that there was no confusion about Marge's faith; all identified her as Christian.

Chapter 6

What My Friends Teach Us About Communication

Close examination of the transcribed interviews with my friends revealed three areas where perception gaps occur that are related directly to communication. The first of these became evident when I looked at which specific topics my friends report as being difficult to communicate to the other group. The second is in how FIWs and PMVs rate overall evaluation of communication. The most dramatic is the third gap area, which I discovered by examining the labels each used to identify individuals.

Topics that are Difficult to Communicate

Muted Group Theory (MGT) tells us, as we have discussed earlier, that different life experiences between the more dominant and less dominant result in muting. So if MGT dynamics apply within the smaller power difference between FIWs and PMVs, it should be expected that my friends perceive some topics as more difficult to talk about with the other due to the FIWs' intimate experiences with incarceration that is not shared with PMVs. And in fact, four topics emerged from this study as being those that my friends identify as difficult to communicate about to the other. These four topics have to do with: communicating the gospel, PMV attitudes about prisoners, the "honesty" issue, and the presence of God in prison.

Communicating the Gospel

The following should alarm anyone in urban mission; my friends the PMVs overwhelmingly report that they have difficulty communicating the gospel message! More than half, fifty-five percent reported this as the most difficult topic to discuss, and forty-six percent cited this as the basis of most misunderstandings. MGT makes the cause obvious. Even the more dominant group admits that differing life experiences exacerbate the situation, as many PMVs voiced difficulty in knowing how to bridge those experiential gaps in order to present the gospel in a meaningful way.

In much of communication, either the more powerful group remains unaware of muting and how it affects the less powerful group, or they find the muting irrelevant. But when the entire purpose for interaction between the two groups is to communicate the life-giving gospel of Jesus Christ, the difficulty of bridging experiential gaps becomes crucial. The outstanding reason for PMVs to enter the prison is to communicate the gospel, and that communicating the gospel is a challenge under any circumstances. Thus, differing life experiences was actually recognized as a cause of misunderstandings by PMVs (23%).

PMVs Attitudes about Prisoners

Not surprising to me, given the power differential dynamics between the two, almost one third of FIWs said that they had difficulty in communicating to PMVs about the PMVs' attitudes towards prisoners. First, in MGT terms, how does the subdominant group make their voices heard by the dominant group? Secondly, it is dangerous for the less powerful to voice displeasure to the powerful. Thirdly, the FIWs perceive that there is a credibility gap. "Because what do we know?" says Eva, laughing with a wry edge. "What do we know? We're prisoners. We're murderers. We don't know anything--in their mind's eye."

The Chaplain voiced an additional perspective during my interview with her. She believes that the reason that prisoners do not directly confront PMVs is out of respect for the position of the volunteers. She puts it this way:

> They do appreciate the volunteers coming in. So, they don't want to cause a discrepancy that they're teaching in front of others, their peers. They like to do it behind closed doors. So, I respect them for that. If they find something that may have been said, they don't confront the volunteer. They come to the Chaplain. And then I will speak to the volunteer about it.

The Chaplain attributes the reticence of prisoners to personally confront and/or correct PMVs to respect. While I can personally attest that respect is one contributing factor, I am also aware that there is another even more important factor: risk. I repeat, it is dangerous for the less powerful to voice displeasure to the powerful.

It is difficult for outsiders to appreciate how much risk is involved in any situation or interaction where FIWs must communicate to others who are more powerful, or how great the gravity of the consequences. I refer back to the literature which informs us that powerlessness is ubiquitous for the incarcerated women[73] and the enormous risk of retribution for simply speaking of the power dynamics

---

[73] Annette M. Mahoney and Carol Ann Daniel, "Bridging the Power Gap: Narrative Therapy with Incarcerated Women." *The Prison Journal*, 86 (2008): 75-88.

that silence them.[74] The risk is not the same for all prisoners, however. Life term prisoners, who by definition have indeterminate sentences, have much more to lose. While for a short-termer even a serious rules infraction has a specific and limited consequence (perhaps the temporary loss of some privilege, or the loss of good time credits towards early release), even these losses are often restored after a subsequent period of good behavior. For a life term prisoner, however, the most minor infraction may easily result in the denial of parole for a decade.

In a personal example of this, I received a CDC 128A (minor rules infraction citation) in 1994 for not rising up from my chair quickly enough for the newly instituted "standing count" procedure. In 2009, then Governor Schwarzenegger reversed the parole board's decision to grant me parole stating that such a recent (15 years at the time) infraction was evidence that I remained a threat and danger to society. Incidentally, this was my only rules violation in thirty years of incarceration.

This understanding of vulnerability is what Ruby is talking about, saying that she was reticent to interact with PMVs because "I tried to keep personal life away for that reason. I wasn't going to risk being written up when they are not providing love, respect, dignity...but they think they are." She further explained, "If we do one thing or say one thing, they can go back and say this and it could cause us to be locked up. It could take away a whole lot from us. It could take away my visits."

---

[74] Michelle Fine and Maria Elena Torre, "Intimate Details: Participatory Action Research in Prison," *Action Research*, 4 (2006): 253-269.

I will attempt here to translate her lovely, lyrical, Ebonic account, loaded with subdominant life experience references, into language that conveys with contextual explanation, how profound the risks that are inherent in PMV/life term prisoner interactions. In prison, visits are sacred. The visiting room is neutral ground precisely because visits are too important for anyone to endanger. But if a prisoner is even charged with a serious disciplinary infraction, she is taken to the "jail" inside the prison while an investigation takes place, during which time she is put on "non-contact visiting status" where visits are limited to one hour by telephone through glass. So even if she is eventually adjudicated not guilty, and her prison record remains clean, she has suffered great loss. And if she is adjudicated guilty, the loss is even greater. In Ruby's words, "It could take away my anything from me, because you scared and you misunderstood something."

It is extremely difficult to convey just how vulnerable and powerless prisoners are. Ruby continues, "So again, you in control so, okay, let me tell you what you want to hear. Cause God forbid if you go back and say anything. If I say anything wrong and you take it like I'm being threatening, then I'm in trouble, because you are in control." She cannot confront or correct PMVs even if they are totally wrong, without risking a catastrophic misunderstanding.

Ruby finishes this topic by adding, "You can say I sneezed and it got on you. And it could be perceived as I spit on you, and I'm in trouble. I might say 'damn,' and you might look at me and be like, 'What did you say?'" These are the reasons that she gives for being "on the defense" or "nervous to death" about daring to correct or confront a PMV.

But it was a PMV, Gordon, who had also been a prisoner at one time, who explained these power issues most vividly. The reason the prisoner cannot confront PMVs about their attitudes is that "when your head is inside the lion's mouth, you don't slap the lion!"

The "Honesty" Issue

What makes this an "honesty issue" is that some FIWs characterize the communication gap between themselves and the PMVs as stemming from dishonesty on the part of the PMVs. Julie describes the issue with honesty this way: "I would like the prison ministers to be more honest about what it is their church or any church they're associated with can give to someone that's come out." This is because, in her experience as an FIW who has looked for assistance, "most times it's not what they say. You know?" What therefore might simply be innocent miscommunication is perceived by Julie to be an intentional act of dishonesty.

Diane shares Julie's belief that there is intentional dishonesty, and attributes it to the attempt at self-aggrandizement by some PMVs. They promise what they wish they could provide instead of what they are actually able to provide to paroling prisoners. She asserts that the "biggest thing is, be honest. Don't proselytize what you're not able to perform." She specifically cited one PMV who, she explained, would stand before "four hundred, five hundred women and say just give us a call and we'll make sure that you have housing," but then failed to follow through when FIWs paroled and contacted the ministry.

The above FIWs perceive that promises of physical assistance have been made to them that were not later forthcoming from the ministries, and label this "dishonest." Most women in prison have had their fill of empty promises. They are not looking to PMVs to provide them with pipe dreams about opportunities. What FIWs are actually asking is for PMVs to give them information from which prisoners are able to form realistic expectations.

A second issue with "honesty" has to do more with the emotional and spiritual realm. Sometimes what FIWs perceive as unkept promises, are simply the well-intentioned hopes of PMVs who are imposing their hopes upon the prisoners they minister to. When the topic of this hope-promise is freedom, and the freedom does not manifest, it is devastating to the prisoner. Tammy relates that she would hear PMVs make promises to other prisoners such as "if you will change your life, God will set you free." But when the gates of prison do not miraculously open, the result can be that "it makes some people retreat backwards, because they're not getting honest answers."

I can attest to how cruel this kind of PMV hopefulness can be. I distinctly remember a whole prison ministry team bringing me up to the front of a service in order to lay hands and pray for me prior to my first parole board hearing in 1989. One woman had what she was certain was a word from God that, if I would have faith, I would be released that very year. The board did grant me parole; however, the date of that parole was set for 1995. And as that date approached, Governor Pete Wilson used his position to request that my parole be rescinded, which it was. I was eventually granted parole by the board eleven times, with well-meaning PMVs assuring me that I was "going home this time," before my eventual release in 2010.

It was brutally difficult to deal with PMVs who accused me of not having faith in a situation where I was trying to be realistic. I needed to be able to emotionally and spiritually survive yet another bitter disappointment. I understood that their words were their projection of love and hope upon me, what Jeremiah warns against in 29:8: "do not listen to the dreams that they dream." I knew that they had no idea how much pain they were causing me.

However, PMV Bev addressed the "honesty" issue from an entirely different perspective. She was amazed that prisoners had taken to heart her assurances that they were able to pass her classes, without having understood the unstated requirements that they would have to actually attend class and do the assigned work. Bev explained that she was volunteering as an instructor in the faith-based program when something "really alerted me to be careful how I express myself." She "with all good faith" expressed to a class that she and her team were there to help, and to ensure that the prisoners succeeded, were able to get through the course, and do well. However, some of the students did not do the work, and therefore did not pass the course. These students considered it Bev's fault that they did not succeed, since she had promised success was possible.

> My thoughts really weren't relating to the reality that they were living. I would say I caused them confusion in a sense, even though they didn't do the work. They were sort of hanging on my expectation, my positive expectation versus the reality that they might not do it.

The dominant U.S. culture holds that success is contingent upon effort, and that anyone who is willing to put in the necessary effort can achieve their goals. It never occurred to Bev that, in some people's life experiences, there is no correlation between effort and success.

One of my FIW friends, Gail, proposes a solution: listening. Yet she has difficulty articulating in dominant language how this would work. She says that if both sides would listen, this could be the mechanism for a phenomenal "repair… fix…glue…flextape, whatever you want to call it, for the inmates." She explained that there is a prerequisite attitude for this listening, that PMVs would "have to be open minded. First you got to be willing, open minded, and honest." Gail even gave an example of what PMVs and prisoners who are both willing to be open to honest communication would sound like:

> "Honey, I honestly don't understand what you've been through or how you've been through, but I'm willing to listen. I'm going to keep it where I may have some resources for you. And I want to be honest about that, because not all resources are available." Bam! [The prisoner will say] "Well, okay, she may be able to help me." There's an open communication and credibility!

This is a commendable suggestion, which I agree should be put into practice more often, but this alone is not sufficient to the issue. Listening is not enough to ensure understanding, especially where there are unrecognized impediments to communication. We must actively come to grips with the hidden issues due to dominant and subdominant group power dynamics.

The Presence of God in Prison

Many missionaries err in believing that they bring Jesus to the mission field. PMVs are not immune to making this error. This is why one difficult topic of communication for FIWs centers around explaining to PMVs that the presence of God is known inside the prison walls. Eva puts it this way; "Jesus lived at CIW when we were there. I don't know about now, but when we was there, Jesus was living at CIW. Amen?!" This tangible presence of Jesus in the prison church is what has caused

Jason S. Sexton to coin the term ecclesia incarcerate to describe this portion of Christ's body.[75]

Ruby eloquently tells the story of her spiritual experience at CIW:

> I was on a retreat for twenty-seven years. And my retreat...um...if I tell you that he would come like, I could feel him physically, his presence, I would feel him all the time...all the time. It used to make me nervous. I was the one that, oh, he always made me nervous because, this is the God of the universe! Why is he in here? Why is he in my room? You know, why do I feel him? You know, okay? Okay. My retreat was like that. The God of the universe was visiting me today in my room. The God of the universe made me so drunk in the Holy Spirit that I didn't know what was going on. My retreat...that he broke up my fallow heart...and he taught me (sobbing).

A little later on in the same interview, Ruby explains how PMVs reacted to her sharing this experience with them:

> Me. Do you have any stories, again, about how prison ministry volunteers misunderstood things that you told them?
>
> Ruby. All the time. (both laugh) Not all of them, but all the time. You know...uh...
>
> Me. Can you give me any examples?
>
> Ruby. The one I just told you about. That...um...I was on a retreat for twenty-seven years. And to feel him all the time. "You may think you feel him all the time."
>
> Me. They said that to you?
>
> Ruby. Yeah. "You may think you feel him all the time." And I said, "Okay."
>
> Me. That took my breath away to hear you say that.
>
> Ruby. Yeah. They say, "You may think you feel him." I say, "I feel him all the time."

---

[75] Jason S. Sexton, "Toward a Prison Theology of California's *ecclesia incarcerate*," *Theology* 118 (2) (2015): 83-91.

This is a profound example of muting. The PMV who had not experienced the ongoing presence of Jesus and the Holy Spirit as manifested within prison walls, did not respect what Ruby communicated. Ruby was left saying "Okay," accepting that her voice was muted. But my personal experience resonates deeply with Ruby's account. It is true. When life is profoundly stark, the presence of God is more visible; the light shines brightest in the dark. Jesus lives at CIW with His prisoners.[76]

Evaluation of Communication

I developed an exercise, a semantic differential, to use in my interview with the intention of rating the overall satisfaction with communication between FIWs and PMVs. What I asked was, "For each pair of words, please mark the box that rates the extent to which you believe this characterizes communication between prisoners and prison ministry volunteers." I then gave them a paper with a seven-point scale between words describing good/positive traits on the left and bad/negative traits on the right. I wanted to see if there was an observable shift between the scoring of the FIWs and the PMVs.

Even a cursory glance at the results of the semantic differential (See Appendix Table 5: "Rating Communication") reveals a shift of oval FIW responses towards the right (negative) and triangle PMV responses towards the left (positive) side in evaluating the overall communication between the two groups. What this tells us is that PMVs perceive communicating with FIWs as a more positive experience than do the FIWs, with three exceptions. PMVs rate communication as both more

---

[76] This is not to say that Jesus imprisons women! Rather, Christian prisoners at CIW see themselves as serving Jesus, and belonging to Him, in contrast to belonging to the State of California.

different and more unclear than do FIWs. The reason for the third exception, an apparent anomaly in scoring the sober-high continuum, is explained by information supplied during the interviews. Several of my PMV friends minister primarily in the CIW psychiatric unit, and many of the women there are highly medicated. Therefore, these PMVs perceive this as a lack of sobriety that impairs the communication process.

In terms of MGT, the dominant group, the PMVs, whose language more closely describes their life experiences, rate communication more positively than do the subdominant FIWs, who are communicating in language that either does not describe their life experiences or is not understood and respected by the dominant group.

One other aspect of overall communication tenor is the actual lack of communication. By this I mean that both some FIWs and some PMVs state that they do not communicate enough, due to time and prison facility restraints, to have actual misunderstandings. This topic will be dealt with in greater detail in Chapter 7 when discussing mentors.

Dehumanizing Labels

It was with horror but not surprise that I recognized the following pattern emerging from the data I was collecting. As I was transcribing interviews, I noticed that some (not all) research subjects from both PMV and FIW groups referred to incarcerated women as "inmates" and everyone else as "people." I decided to look into this further.

The computer software I was using for analyzing the interview transcripts, MAXQDA, had an option for performing an Extended

Lexical Search. What this meant was that I was able to choose a word, such as "inmate," and search through the entire body of study interviews to see how many times this word was used and by whom. The results of my searches confirmed my observations. Some of my friends demonstrate in their speech a perceptual dichotomy in which "inmates" and "people" are mutually exclusive groups.

I deliberately refrain from referring to the women at CIW as "inmates" even though this is the term most often used within the bureaucratic written format system at CIW. More to the point, I refrain from referring to the women at CIW as "inmates" specifically because "inmate" is the term most often used. Through the decades that I was incarcerated, 1980 through 2010, the California Department of Corrections and Rehabilitation (CDCR) slowly became more sensitive to offensive or derogatory terms of address, especially to women, and even to prisoners.[77] While in the early 1980s it was not uncommon for Correctional Officers (COs) to address women prisoners with such terms as "bitches," or "whores," such forms of address have not been tolerated within CDCR for the past couple of decades. Currently, COs[78] are directed to refer to and address female prisoners in a group as "ladies" and individuals by "Inmate (last name)." Prisoners are also directed to use the label "inmate" in any formal bureaucratic communication. If I was at my prison job and needed to answer an inmate-access

---

[77] If you find these words confusing, it is because you have not experienced that "women" are "people" but prisoners are not. It was a process for the term "sexual harassment" to enter dominant group language and be applied first to women in general, and later extended to women prisoners.

[78] Just as "Inmate" or "I/m" is the official title for prisoners, "Correctional Officer" or "CO" is the official title for staff, written or verbal. COs prefer to be addressed as such and bridle when outsiders refer to them as "guards." This is, after all, the vocabulary as defined and mandated by the CDCR, the dominant group.

institutional telephone, I was required to say "Inmate Smith speaking." There is even an official abbreviation, I/m, for the word inmate.

The issue this presents is that "inmate" has a connotation of someone who is less than human. It is not only the fact that, because of incarceration, prisoners have forfeited some basic rights such as freedom of movement, the right to vote, and the right to bear arms, to name a few. Beyond that, one simply does not treat human beings the dehumanizing way that "inmates" are all too often treated. I confronted this issue directly in my interview with Ruby:

Me.	I have another question, about, 'cause you said several times…um…that they need to realize that we are human beings.
Ruby.	Yeah!
Me.	Do you…did you come out of prison feeling like you really were a human being?
Ruby.	That is so difficult to answer.
Me.	That's why I'm asking it.
Ruby.	I don't even know what I felt like when I stepped out. Um…
Me.	My perspective is, you don't treat a human being the way they treated us, so I must not be human.
Ruby.	Like that! But again, I'm trying to tell, that's why I'm trying to tell you. What am I? Do you get what I'm saying to you? Like, I don't know…I don't know what I am. Um…what I…let me out of here.

A few minutes later the same Ruby clarified what the term "inmate" signifies for her, that it is a form of "…like brainwash. You an inmate…inmate…inmate…inmate… inmate…inmate."

Another FIW, Marsha, wished she could address PMVs to explain to them "You're not dealing with prisoners. That's it. You're not dealing with prisoners. It's the human being, God's creature, God's creation, that you're dealing with."

Literature provides other examples of this attitude. Researchers interviewing a woman at a California prison documented her explanation that "they don't treat [you] as human, you know? You're just another inmate. You're a piece of dirt."[79]

Some PMVs are very aware of this issue. Cindy explains, "It doesn't matter if you're incarcerated or not. They're still people...just human." Nevertheless, several of my friends do consistently contrast "inmates" with "people." In one instance Grace, a PMV, explicitly argues the equality of all, yet only uses the word "people" to refer to outsiders, and "inmate" to refer to insiders. "Oh, the church on the inside, the people on the outside don't have a clue what it's like to be an inmate."

There is one more way this topic is addressed by my friends during interviews, but indirectly. The term "less than" without any subsequent comparative, leaves the comparison to the listener to fill in. Thus, while the overt intent may well be "less than" some other person, as when FIW Tammy says, "I would feel less than them, not as powerful," the underlying message in the prison context is "less than human."

PMV Judy struggles with how to combat this issue.

> And they have a very hard time with that, because they're having to pay the price of their sin, a lot of times, so it's hard to figure, it's hard to understand, it's forgiven as far as the Lord is concerned. But there's still paying the penalty that the world has given them. It's hard for them to separate that. They continue to think that they're, that they're less than because of that, a majority of them.

---

[79] Mike Vuolo and Candace Kruttschitt, "Prisoners' Adjustment, Correctional Officers, and Context: The Foreground and Background of Punishment in Late Modernity." *Law and Society Review* 42 (2) (2008): 330.

We're all the same, and I think they understood that I under...that I felt that way. I hope that they know. They're not, again that word, they're not less than. And I see so many people, COs included, who treat them less than. And, I just want to tell them God doesn't.

However, notice Judy's word choices here. Prisoners are referred to by third person pronouns: they, them, the ones. This is in contrast to "people, COs included" who actively do the dehumanizing. She sees that prisoners feel "less than" but does not realize that her word and label choices are contributing to the problem she is trying to solve.

The FIWs do not always notice the link between perception and word choice either. We must remember that for the subdominant group member to effectively communicate she must use the dominant language. One example is FIW Gail who frequently uses the term "people" to refer to prisoners. Still, she felt the need to correct herself during our interview saying, "that person is already, the inmate is already" in order to differentiate who she was referring to, that she was humanizing the prisoner rather than referring to a non-prisoner.

FIW Diane explained to me, "But I have been told that they felt that I was a very strong-willed person. One almost said minded inmate." A little later on in our conversation, I came back to this and asked for clarification.

> Me. You talked about the difference between being called a strong-willed person and the look on your face when you said, "strong-minded inmate." Could you explain that look on your face?
> Diane. Absolutely.
> Me. For the record...
> Diane. Absolutely. Because when the person said that, it let me know that she viewed me as just a number, just a person who was incarcerated, who happened to

>   be strong-willed. And what I wanted to convey was, when do you take us out of the category of the "inmate" mentality.
> Me.   She's putting quote marks in the air around inmate. (laughing)
> Diane. Yes! I am putting quote marks around that! And empower us to be individual women of God.

I emphasize that this dichotomy of inmates/people serves to ingrain in the prisoner population that "inmates" are not fully persons. Due to differing life experiences, prisoners are extremely sensitive to dehumanization in ways that PMVs are not. Thus, the communication gap here is the degree to which the term "inmate" is dehumanizing.

Denominations

There is very little denominational division or loyalty at CIW. The idea of denominations is downplayed in the extreme in prisons. Most prisoners have rudimentary, if any, understanding of what makes denomination important for so many Christians. In all actuality, it is the denominational identity of the chaplain that has most meaning to the prisoners, and that changes with each chaplain. Additionally, PMVs are specifically prohibited from proselytizing or in any way elevating one denomination over another. Prisoners might know which church a particular team represents, or which church specific volunteers are affiliated with. However, it is often the case in the prison environment that even this basic information is not available. Add to this that there may be thirty different groups giving services and Bible studies in a given month, it is not so surprising that denominational distinctions have less meaning for prisoners than for the general population outside prison.

In my case, until recently I called myself a Pentecostal Lutheran although I am now under care towards ordination by the Christian Church (Disciples of Christ), my husband identifies as a Mennonite although he grew up in a Baptist church, my sister-in-law's family is Eastern Orthodox, and I am a member of the Evangelical Missiological Society. Denominational differences have little meaning to me or to my FIW friends. But I personally found this to be a disadvantage when doing seminary coursework. I simply could not understand what the big deal was.

This issue with denominations is closely tied to my discussion in the previous chapter of CIW as a centered set church. When the criterion for church membership is not based on creeds, doctrines, manner of baptism, or preferred style of worship, as they are for bounded set churches, then those criteria lose importance. Thus, those of us who are spiritually raised in a centered set church have a difficult time imagining any other criteria for membership than of direction and movement towards Jesus as our center. But what is a positive attribute of the CIW church in terms of unity, often has negative repercussions for FIWs upon parole.

My research shows that the lack of denominational understandings is a phenomenon at CIW that is a source of false expectations. Diane explained how not understanding denominations impacted her as well as other FIWs. While still inside prison, she had accepted a job as Associate Pastor for Prison Ministry from a specific PMV. But when she actually attended the church outside, she was shocked to find out it was Seventh Day Adventist, and her "spirit rejected it." Diane explained that other FIWs confided to her that they "felt the same way I felt, but did not have the boldness" to confront the situation. It was only years later, after earning a Masters of Divinity degree, that Diane began to be "concerned that so many other people were being persuaded into the different kinds of theology without being given a choice to choose if that's where they wanted to go."

The significance to FIWs can be understood by Carol's experience after leaving prison. When I asked if she was currently attending a church she had replied in the negative. She said she had tried several churches, but had not been able to find any that really welcomed her, or that suited her worship needs. "Do you remember Nigel?" she asked me. "I really enjoyed the services his team provided. I wish I could find a church like that!" What she did not know is that Nigel was part of a Vineyard team, that Vineyard is a denomination, and that she was looking for a church with Pentecostal worship practices. But now she has given up, and is not ready to risk rejection and disappointment again. There is a consequence to not understanding denominations.

It was during my interview with the Chaplain that I first began to connect my own issues in understanding what the various denominations stood for with how denominationalism was, or was not, communicated to us by PMVs. Had there not been a last-minute issue with bureaucratic paperwork, there were seven prisoners who would have been ordained in 2010, while still incarcerated at CIW, under the auspices of the Chaplain's denomination, AME. I was one of those prisoners, and had no idea what being ordained AME meant other than my then being allowed to serve communion to fellow prisoners. The Chaplain explains that she specifically instructs volunteers to not proselytize or in any way put down another denomination or faith. She explained, "In other words, we do not go against another religion there at the prison."

Some PMVs, by using the name of their church in their ministry team name, give prisoners a clue as to what denominational affiliation the team has. Others give clues with their practices, such as Pentecostal speaking in tongues, healings, and deliverance ministries. Some teams are specifically nondenominational. PMVs do note that a "good" church should have a style consistent with its denomination. However, this becomes a very unclear issue, clouding prisoner understandings of denominations, which does not help when, upon parole, it is time to choose a church.

Chapter 7

What is Going on with Power?

Power dynamics are what Muted Group Theory (MGT) and this book are all about. This is not a subject that dominant group, egalitarian, North Americans are all that comfortable with. Looking down from the top, power issues are often invisible. But looking up from the bottom, often all one can see is affected by power dynamics. This is probably the biggest lesson that I learned in my thirty years of incarceration, and is why power dynamics are the core of this work.

In this chapter I will be discussing three particular perception gaps relating to power dynamics between FIWs and PMVs. My research data confirms gaps related to: (1) PMV discomfort with power, (2) PMV and FIW perceptions regarding prisoner power, and (3) FIW perception of not being listened to.

But first, I will share a story that will provide background for what is to follow. Power is not evil. In fact, I will argue at the end of this chapter that shared power is an answer to many of the issues we have examined in this book so far. However, power that is ignored is problematic. And power that is abused is catastrophic. The following is my personal account of a situation in the church at CIW where power was abused.

Abuse of Power

Prior to the gracious female Protestant Chaplain whose words are interspersed within these pages, CIW had a long chain of male Protestant Chaplains with varying degrees of effectiveness. While it is good to give wounded female prisoners a positive male role model, there are inherent dangers with crossing gender boundaries. The last male chaplain proves this point. I will refer to him as Chaplain Don.

This issue was that Chaplain Don was a sexual predator who was put in a position of spiritual and custodial power over wounded women with very little personal power. I do not make these charges lightly. I personally made a sexual harassment complaint to the then existing prison administration.

However, I was not a targeted victim of his. He was interested in petite blonde women, and he specifically chose to prey on women with known psychiatric conditions. After all, power and credibility are generally positively correlated; these were women with no power and even less credibility. By this time in my incarceration, I did have some credibility as an elder in the prison church who ministered in the psychiatric unit. At the same time, I worked in the psychiatric unit as a CIW Mental Health Department Peer Helper. (We could not be called Peer Counselors since we were not licensed. We were thus only allowed to listen, inform, support, teach, and otherwise help our sister prisoners. We did not counsel.) It was natural that I was the first person that these women approached in order to ask for help.

In October 1994, I made my formal complaint to the Associate Warden, telling him of both the unwanted touching and stroking that I had been the recipient of, as well as the complaints of several of the women I ministered to. These women knew that they had no credibility and feared repercussions from both the Chaplain and of custody staff if they were seen as troublemakers. Chaplain Don countered with the argument that I just did not like him because he had considered giving my ministry to a different prisoner.

The irony here is that Chaplain Don actually did not actually make that threat to me until after I had reported him. If I did not rescind my accusations against him, he said, then he would remove me from my position as elder. He also threatened to write those small disciplinary memos that could be so devastating in a parole board hearing not only on me, but also on the other prisoner members of the psychiatric ministry team.

It was two years later, in 1996, that Chaplain Don was caught in the act by the CIW institutional investigation team, and fired. Here is the account as presented in All Too Familiar: Sexual Abuse of Women in U.S. State Prisons, a book published in 1996 by the Human Rights Watch:

> In 1995 the Post-Conviction Justice Project at the University of Southern California filed a lawsuit against the Protestant chaplain and his supervisors at the California Institute for Women.[80] The suit alleges that the chaplain sexually assaulted female prisoners, thus violating the eighth amendment's prohibition against cruel and unusual punishment. In addition, the suit asserts that women prisoners were afraid to worship with the chaplain and thus, their freedom of religion was infringed. Although some prisoners reported the sexual assaults to prison staff in October 1994, no action was taken against the chaplain until February 1996. At that time, subsequent to the filing of the lawsuit in October

---

[80] Dorothy Q. Thomas et al., "*All Too Familiar: Sexual Abuse Of Women In U.S. State Prisons,*" *Human Rights Watch*. Citing *Patterson v. Deshores*, Civil Action File No. EDCV-95-397, First Amended Complaint, October 31, 1995 (1996).

1995, the chaplain was barred from the prison, but only after he reportedly assaulted another woman.[81]

This is muting, but on a grand and deliberate scale. The "#MeToo" movement is one of women finding their voices and refusing to be muted, but this incident was occurring over twenty years prior to that, before the term "sexual harassment" was fully accepted by the dominant culture, especially the dominant male culture. Therefore, the muting of women reporting sexual violence was occurring at a structural level.

Here was a woman, a prisoner, suffering from mental health issues, who had gone to the Chaplain to ask for help in restoring her relationship to her daughter. He said he could help, but then demanded a price, in sexual favors. It is bad enough that my reporting was not acted upon. But during the discovery portion of the lawsuit proceedings, the attorneys for the woman who sued both the Chaplain and the State were informed that no record of my report of Chaplain Don's misconduct could be found. My friend and ministry partner Marge, whose funeral some years later is described in Chapter 5, also had reported Chaplain Don's misconduct, and her report was also not to be found. These details are important for reasons in addition to the obvious injustice. The implications of how MGT power dynamics play out are hidden within this account of subdominant group life experiences.

Because our reports were not produced for the attorneys at discovery, Marge and I were asked if we would be willing to testify in court. We said, "Yes." But structural muting means that there was

---

[81] Thomas et al., "All Too Familiar" Telephone interview: Carrie Hempel, professor of law, University of Southern California Law School, March 6, 1996 (1996).

immense pressure on us to not testify, and huge negative repercussions for us if we did. For a prisoner to testify in court, she must be transported from CIW to the county jail and housed there for the duration of the case. If a prisoner is Out To Court (OTC) for longer than three days, her personal property is packed up, secured in storage, and her bed is given to someone else. What this would mean to me is that someone, hopefully my cellmate who I trusted, would go through absolutely everything I own and pack it up in boxes. Upon returning to CIW, it would likely take two weeks for my property to be reissued to me, and then only after being searched, item by item, to ensure that there was no contraband, such as an extra plastic bowl for cooking or too many pairs of socks. In the meanwhile, I would not automatically be relocated to my former cell with my former cellmate, and would be losing the comfort of that relationship. I would also have lost not only my job, but also my classification standing as a full-time worker. This means that I would not be allowed phone calls or to shop on canteen. It usually takes a month for an OTC return to be reclassified and reinstated to her job, if the job is still available. This is, in MGT language, loss of societal benefits.

  The above is just the loss suffered at the CIW end. Transportation to court has its own prices and humiliations. To leave CIW I would have to be secured in chains. My ankles would be cuffed and chained together. I would also wear a waist chain that secured my wrists to my side. And then I would be bussed to county jail, where I would be housed as a high-security prisoner. I would then be taken back and forth to court, spending my days in a bare court holding cell that contained merely a toilet, a sink, and a bench to sit on. I would be enduring all of this in hope that I would be heard in court, that the judge and/or jury would give credibility to a chained prisoner. The defense attorney's job would be to convince the court to discount my testimony, to mute me, by pointing out my lack of credibility as a prisoner. I would be forced to relive the trauma of my encounters with Chaplain Don, and that in his presence. Additionally, it would be certain to trigger the trauma of being in a courtroom, with no power or voice, when I was convicted of murder for not protecting my daughter from the man who beat her to death.

To Marge's and my great relief, the resulting lawsuit was eventually settled out of court, with the State of California paying damages to the plaintiff. We did not have to testify. As a result of the State being forced to pay a cost, there was a difference, and changes were made. The State could no longer afford to mute the voices of prisoners who alleged sexual misconduct by free persons. All reports of sexual misconduct must now be fully investigated.

This is a worst-case account of power dynamics and muting in prison. My reasons for sharing this painful episode are two-fold. First, it was a culmination of my prison experiences such as these that made me realize the insidious nature of the interplay of power between prisoners and non-prisoner. It is for this reason that I found myself drawn to MGT. Secondly, Chaplain Don did not limit his unwanted attentions to prisoners. Several female PMVs, after he was caught and fired, admitted to me that he had made uncomfortable comments and unwanted sexual overtures to them. These PMVs were also muted. Chaplain Don had the power and resources to deny them entry to the prison. If they did not want to suffer the loss of their ministry opportunities, if they did not want to leave the women prisoners and their spiritual needs to this man, they had to accept their own muting.

This is the setting in which FIWs and PMVs are interacting. Power issues permeate the very fabric of prison. What follows is, thankfully, not as dramatic or traumatic. However, whether the power dynamics are acknowledged or not, they exist and they impact the relationships between FIWs and PMVs.

PMVs Discomfort with Power

FIWs believe that PMVs have power; PMVs minimize or deny the power difference.

One of the more interesting, and surprising to me, results of talking with my PMV friends was the realization that many of them are uncomfortable with discussing power. Power issues and labeling are central issues to my work with MGT especially because they go towards defining the dominant and subdominant groups. And the reason that defining who is dominant, and who is subdominant, matters so much is because both groups tend to minimize the distance between them. What I have come to realize is that the actual distance between the two groups is exponentially greater than either group is willing to acknowledge, but especially on the part of the PMVs.[82]

Most people will readily agree that there is a significant power differential at work in interactions between prisoner and custody staff. My FIW friends are universal in their understanding that PMVs have more power than prisoners, even if it is not as much power as custody staff has. As Ruby stated unequivocally, "It's still power."

---

[82] Anatolij Dorodnych and Anna Kuzio, "The Role of Cultural Scripts and Contextualization Cues in Intercultural (Mis)communication." In *Intercultural Miscommunication Past and Present*, edited by Kryk-Kastovsky. Frankfurt, GE: Peter Lang, Internationaler Verlag der Wissenschaften, 2012, 95.

However, I was surprised to realize that many of the PMVs did not understand how much power they had, or the importance of the power they had in comparison to prisoners. One PMV adamantly exclaimed that she did not have more power than prisoners, "Well, except for that part we have the keys and can walk out, no there's no power difference. And anyway, I don't run my prison ministry that way."

I wanted to explore power dynamics by looking not only at whether my PMV friends felt powerful, but how they felt about being powerful. In Table 2, "Perception of Power by PMVs", we see the responses by PMVs to the two connected questions "Do you think you are perceived as powerful when you interact with prison inmates?" and "How does that make you feel?" Interestingly, only sixty-one percent of the PMVs admit to being perceived as powerful; thirty-nine percent do not admit to being perceived as powerful. Looking at this from a slightly different angle, sixty-seven percent either denied power altogether or made comments that revealed a distinct discomfort with being perceived as powerful using such words as "not comfortable," "conflicted," and "embarrassed." And those who did not voice discomfort used such words as "appreciated," "humbled," and "respected" to describe how they felt.

In addition to the oral interviews, as I mentioned earlier, both PMVs and FIWs participated in some written activities, one of which, the Likert Scale, is relevant here (see Table 5 "Rating of Communication"). I had used this activity in hopes it would show a difference in how my FIW friends and my PMV friends perceived their personal power. I asked each of my friends to rate, on a five-point scale, how powerful they felt in comparison to persons of twenty different statuses. However, I initially found the Likert Scale to be unfruitful in trying to establish any differences in perception of personal power, since both FIWs and PMVs had issues with this exercise due to my unclear directions. I tried revising the directions in an attempt to ameliorate these difficulties, but I did not believe I was very successful. Thus, while I still presented the Likert Scale activity at each interview, since it generated conversation about interactions with subgroups, I initially believed that collating the results did not produce usable data.

It was only in revisiting the results of the Likert Scale at a later date that I realized its value. The reason that I could not tease out a difference is the very important fact that they did not perceive a difference. Entirely consistent with their verbal responses, the Likert Scale reveals that PMVs do not perceive themselves as more powerful than FIWs. PMVs and FIWs rated themselves with striking similarity. In other words, the PMVs rated themselves as having the same degree of relative power as prisoners.

Betty, unlike most of the other PMVs, has a better understanding of her power and what it means. She not only says she has power, but she believes that it is necessary for her to have power. Betty says she should be perceived as having power because PMVs should "have power enough to help them." She also acknowledges that PMV power is necessary "because they [prisoners] are powerless, somehow. And because we are free." She makes one more important point about prisoners and power, that "they could be really powerful." Another word for this is advocacy. Advocacy involves sharing power and using the advocate's power to empower those being oppressed. Prisoners are looking for PMVs to be advocates, not equals in power.

Perceptions Regarding Prisoner Power

PMVs believe that FIWs have power; FIWs do not agree.

To my questions regarding misunderstandings between FIWs and PMVs, several of my friends gave responses that centered on power issues. To build on the previous paragraph, many prisoners are looking to PMVs as advocates in order to find and obtain personal empowerment. However, when it comes to prisoners and power, on one hand PMVs overestimate the power a prisoner has, particularly in terms of access to and relationships with their children (see Table 1 "Summary of Difficult to Explain Spiritual Topics).

On the other hand, when prisoners are successfully being empowered, some PMVs interpret this as prisoners exerting too much power. Diane addressed this, explaining that when the Chaplain allows prisoners to be in leadership positions, PMVs think that "the women just have too much power." However, Diane maintains, "It had nothing to do with that. You're being empowered to mature."

Gordon, a PMV who himself had prior personal experience with being incarcerated, talked about PMV and FIW power, but only in terms of spiritual power imbued by the Holy Spirit. His actions during our interview, however, were in contrast to his words. This same man made repeated power assertions during the interview, and a considerable portion of our interview involved his efforts to assert and maintain dominance over and maintain control of the interview. He challenged my education. He made comments such as, "What idiot came up with that question?"[83] and "That question doesn't make any sense." He made a major point of determining our relative ages, since, as my senior, this

---

[83] Of course, the "idiot" he was referring to was me. Nevertheless, I did not correct him when he presumed it was something a professor had mandated.

gave him precedence over me. If he exerted his power with me, I have to wonder what the power dynamics are like when he is interacting with prisoners at CIW.

Another issue with FIW power emerges when PMVs were asked "Do you think there are any significant manifestations of power contrasts when prisoners and prison ministry volunteers communicate with each other?" Almost half of PMVs who answered in the affirmative, identify prisoners as being solely in power, while FIWs say this is the case zero percent of the time. Further, seventy percent of PMVs perceive prisoners as having some power, while only thirty percent of FIWs believe that this is true.

However, a close look at some of the PMV replies to the question "Do you think there are any significant manifestations of power contrasts when prisoners and prison ministry volunteers communicate with each other?" reveals the underlying issue. PMVs confuse aggression with power. Betty says that those prisoners that disagree with their message "take us on," while Lisa explained that "like they do in the hood" that prisoners have "a tendency to push." Sally calls it "resistance." There is a proverb that even a mouse will attack a cat when it is cornered. Aggression, which is being perceived by PMVs as prisoner power, may well be what we discussed earlier in Chapter 2 as the angrily disengaged response of a muted subdominant group member.

Finally, yet one more hidden power reveals itself from within the pile sort activity regarding what churches provide. Two-thirds, sixty-seven percent, of the PMVs believe that paroling women ***sometimes find dignity*** in outside churches, while almost half (47%) of FIWs state that churches ***never provide dignity***. The concept of dignity relates to power. The powerful are treated with dignity, often because they demand it. However, the powerless often cannot demand dignity, and therefore are not generally granted it. The same can be said for *the element respect*, where sixty-eight percent of PMVs believe paroling women receive it *sometimes*, but less than half (47%) of FIWs state that paroling women *receive respect sometimes* and twenty percent state that they *receive respect never*.

"They Don't Listen to Us!"

FIWs do not believe that PMV's are listening to them.

One complaint about PMVs that is repeated throughout the FIW interviews is that "they don't listen to us." I asserted earlier, in Chapter 6 about communication, that listening alone is not enough to ensure understanding where unrecognized impediments to communication exist. Still, listening is the requisite first step. But what happens if the powerless cannot get the powerful to listen? Rosa explains in broken English, "It's hard on me to explain to them because they are not understand it. Or they don't want to hear it. That's it." Ruby calls it "crazy," saying, "That's exactly how it is when we're communicating with them. We smile. The smiles are not real. They're not listening." Kathy says of women in prison, "They need some…somebody to hear them." She then says to the PMVs, "If you're going to go in with closed ears and preconceived ideas…then you're not going to be effective."

Eva agrees that this is an issue, "They're not listening." She believes it is because PMVs are "stuck in a place" where they "don't want to hear it." Eva wishes that PMVs understood that from her perspective. "You might want to come and teach me about Jesus…but you're not teaching me about Jesus. You're teaching me about you. And then, when I try to tell you, you don't want to hear it because you know it all."

Gail explains that there were certain topics that PMVs especially refused to listen to.

> Okay. So, not say for me personally, but women who have had trouble with their sexual identity or if they had a girlfriend, it was a complete stop because it was like taboo conversation. And you can't help somebody without listening. And if you're not willing to hear, or you automatically have a predisposed thought pattern on what should/should not be, then it stops the face-to-face talking.

This is the ultimate in muting; even when you speak, no one is listening. As stated above, it results in "a complete stop" and "it stops the face-to-face talking" because the powerful do not have to, and often cannot be made to, listen. I will discuss this more in terms of Muted Group Theory (MGT) in the next chapter.

The Difference Between PMVs and Mentors

PMVs are a distinct category of volunteers who provide church services, bible studies, and events, and are not to be confused with mentors and mentoring programs who foster one-on-one relationships between prisoners and volunteers. While PMVs do admirable work and are indispensable to the church at CIW, they are severely limited in how much direct contact and individual communication they have with Christian prisoners.

Mentoring, which has been identified in academic literature as promising but underutilized by prisons,[84] has been implemented at CIW at various times. Prison Fellowship Life Plan Seminars sought to establish mentoring relationships between volunteers and prisoners during the year prior to release. Over several decades, beginning in the 1970s, first M-2 (Match 2) and later ASK Mentoring (Ask, Seek, Knock) matched prisoners at CIW with religious volunteers who visited, corresponded, and established positive relationships.

The following reveals the value with which FIWs regard mentors:

Ruby. They're not listening. You know who's better? Remember when we used to have the Match Two?
Me. Yes.
Ruby. They were totally different type of people. Some of them believed in God wholeheartedly. They quit the program just to build relationships, to come and pray.
Me. I still see my ASK mentor all the time.
Ruby. Mine passed away. I never got another one.

But even more importantly, my FIW friend Kathy credits her not having communication issues to her relationship with her mentor.

Me. Do you have any stories about how prison ministry volunteers have misunderstood things that you have told them?

---

[84] Matthew A. Koschmann and Brittany L. Peterson,"Rethinking Recidivism: A Communication Approach to Prisoner Reentry." *Journal of Applied Social Science* 7 (22) (2013): 188-207; Mark Brown and Stuart Ross,"Mentoring, Social Capital and Desistance: A Study of Women Released from Prison." *The Australian and New Zealand Journal of Criminology* 43 (1) (2010): 31-50; Byron R. Johnson, "Religious Programs and Recidivism Among Former Inmates in Prison Fellowship Programs: A Long-Term Follow-Up Study." *Justice Quarterly* 21 (2) (2004): 329-354; Carolyn Leitzell, Natalie Madrazo and Caren Warner-Robbins, "Meeting the Gap and Implications for Public Health Professionals." *Home Health Care Management & Practice* 23 (3): 168-175.

> Kathy. No. I don't because I was blessed, very fortunate, to have Angela as my spiritual volunteer who came in to visit me. She was definitely filled with the Holy Spirit and there was nothing that I had to explain to her. When I shared my experiences with her, she was fully, fully understanding; totally on board. She recognized what was really a true experience and not just in my head. You know, she didn't pooh-pooh any idea I had or roll her eyes at anything I had to say concerning something I might have experienced or whatever.

Whether the prisoner participated in the M-2 program or ASK, the relationships developed in this context were very different than what usually developed during church services. First of all, prisoner and volunteer spent considerable time together, a contractual minimum of once a month and often several hours at a time, in one-on-one interpersonal communication and building relationship. In this context, and unlike interactions with PMVs, it was expected that both prisoner and volunteer/mentor would share personal information. Finally, it was intended that these relationships continue after the release of the prisoner. None of these factors were usually present in regular PMV/prisoner interactions at CIW. The lack of time and access for such relationship building was frequently mentioned by PMVs during their interviews as an issue in their communication with prisoners.

I personally know the value of having an ASK Mentor. My Mentor visited me at CIW for several hours at least once a month for a decade, and established a relationship with me while I was in prison. It was my Mentor who heard my heart's desire to attend graduate school someday, found the Fuller Theological Seminary Certificate of Christian Study program, and enrolled me as a distance-learning student. My Mentor waited at the prison gate with a long-stemmed rose to welcome me to the free world upon my release, and she has actively mentored me ever since. She has become more than my friend, she has become part of my family. This research project would not have been possible without all the ways that my Mentor heard me and supported me for the last eighteen years.

Heartbreakingly, the mentoring programs at CIW have expired due to lack of support and funding.

What Prisoners and FIWs Have to Offer

One thing that church members on the outside of the prison walls have difficulty in conceptualizing is that prisoners have much to offer them. As a result of the dominant group, in MGT terms, not respecting the language of the subdominant, language that comes out of their life experiences, the dominant group has difficulty comprehending the gifts that exist within the subdominant life experiences. I am discussing this under the topic of power for two reasons. One, muting of gifts in this way is the result of the dominant group exercising power. Two, the gifts of the subdominant, in this case FIW, group are a form of power and empowerment.

One example of this is the Good Shepherd Lutheran Church case study, which will be presented in Chapter 9, provides emphasis to the interview findings in evidencing the gifts that FIWs have to offer the churches outside of prison. Most prison ministry volunteers focus their ministerial concerns upon the prison and do not bring the prison back to the congregation. But it is when the prison is introduced back to the congregation that changes can begin, and that bridge-building relationships occur. My presence at GSLC put a nonthreatening face to the concept of "prisoner" which helped dominant group church members to open themselves to hearing what prisoners have to say and offer.

For one thing, it is unlikely that the former prisoner takes God's grace, mercy, or freedom for granted. Skeptics frequently view prison conversion "as an inmate's insincere attempt to demonstrate that she has indeed been rehabilitated" while still acknowledging that, for some women prisoners, spiritual knowledge and development contributes to desired changes in their emotional lives.[85] The less skeptical recognize that a woman prisoner may undergo profound conversion experiences in prison that bring about a quantum change in the trajectory of her life and that her testimony can affect the lives of others.[86]

I will share what is, to me, a very small example of how a prisoner's experience can inform the church in a positive way. I have literally experienced being shackled in leg irons and waist chains, as I described in the earlier Chapter 7 regarding "What's Going on With Power." Chains are heavy on the body and the soul. They leave bruises on wrists and ankles, as well as the psyche. I once scolded a young male CO as he escorted several of us prisoners from CIW at the local hospital where we had been transported for medical appointments. The people in the crowded waiting room were already staring at us, some with pity, some with disgust, and yet others with fear, as we shuffled two-by-two across the room, shackled at ankle and waist. This CO was renowned for his immature sense of humor. He thought it was funny to announce, loudly, "Dead Man Walking!" as he escorted us. I was accustomed to

---

[85] Kimberly Greer, "Walking an Emotional Tightrope: Managing Emotions in a Women's Prison." *Symbolic Interaction* 25 (1) (2002):131.

[86] Tom P. O'Connor and Jeff B. Duncan, "The Sociology of Humanist, Spiritual, and religious Practice in Prison: Supporting Responsivity and Desistance from Crime." *Religions* 2 (2011): 594.

both his humor and the humiliation of medical transport, but the woman next to me almost crumpled from the shame.

All this to say, when I sing songs of praise that contain lines about God "breaking the chains that bind us," and that "Jesus set me free!" it is with the above in mind. I am filled with a joyful abandon that insists I raise my hands above my head, a motion that is impossible in chains, to express my gratitude. Yes, there are figurative chains of pain, addiction, and illness, to name a few, that Jesus delivers us from. But these are metaphorical. I have been set free from real iron chains. I have been thanked for pointing out the above, for what this brings to help my sisters and brothers in Christ have a deeper appreciation of his love.

Another value of the prisoner or FIW to the church is that prisoners are an unambiguous proclamation of God's salvation grace, and therefore challenge the church to believe in redemption. To my question "Have you noticed any differences between how prisoners and prison ministry volunteers talk about church?" Ruby explains that prisoners "talk about demonstrations of Holy Spirit," while Maria tells us that "women in prison are more passionate about their faith." God has trained prisoners and FIWs to be boundary crossers and missionaries. At CIW, as State of California employees, Christian staff members are not free to proselytize or proclaim their faith. It may be politically incorrect in many public arenas to proclaim Jesus, or even say "God bless you." But no walls exist that prohibit prisoners from evangelizing to the Correctional Officers, as the story I described in Chapter 5 about the conversion of Officer Mendez made clear.

Chapter 8

Where does this leave MGT?

Now that we have examined what my friends had to say regarding the church, communications, and power, it is time to reexamine MGT. Chapter 2 explained the mechanics of MGT, but now we will see how these mechanics play out in the actual communication dynamics between FIWs and PMVs, one tenet at a time.

Tenet #1 – Creating Language

> *The dominant group creates the language of power and policy based on their life experiences.*

My research clearly shows that PMVs and FIWs are aware that their life experiences are different from that of the other. PMVs explain how different the prison experience is. Bev called it a "very…strange environment to walk into as a volunteer." Cindy says it is because "their world is totally different." While Sally noted that "there's some basic barriers that have to do with their background and their experiences." Jean called it "a whole different perspective" while admitting that "It's hard for me, and I don't understand where they're at." But it was Janet who comes closest to defining the real issue, that "it takes a long time" to "sometimes even actually get that you don't get what they're talking about."

While FIWs agree that there are differing life experiences, they do not always identify these differences quite the same way that PMVs do. Kathy's perspective is that, when she paroled, she "was stuck in a whole different world." Others gave more specific reasons. Carol brought up the issue of sexual abuse, that unless PMVs have "actually been through it themselves" they are not going to understand the profound effect it has upon the victim. Gail says the same thing about drug abuse: "If you haven't withdrawn from drugs, you really don't know the experience and how could you help me with that experience if you really don't know?"

"I don't blame the volunteers," Maria explained graciously, "Because it is very difficult to relate…it's another experience. It's like another world in there."

At the same time, the FIWs had difficulty in articulating what this other world entailed. Some, like Jane, gave up without trying, "Until you've been there, you can never really understand what it's like." Clara stumbled over her words, "they really couldn't comprehend it. They couldn't comprehend why staff treated us like…there are certain things they couldn't comprehend." Clara admitted the difficulty was "that little part that you can't hardly explain, you know. Things affect you. You're not going to be that same person anymore."

The dominant language is not adequate for expressing what FIWs have experienced. When Clara couldn't find the words to finish her sentence above, about "why staff treated us like…" she made eye contact with me and shrugged. She knew I had shared the experience, and that she was able therefore to communicate to me what dominant language did not have words for. For lack of a better term, I call it dehumanization; it is "why staff treated us like" we were not human beings. Yet this is only a mild approximation of what Clara is talking about.

What both FIWs and PMVs do agree upon is that prison is an experience outside the range of PMV comprehensions. Further, the backgrounds that lead women to prison are also likely to be outside the range of PMV experiences. Rephrased in the words of MGT, the dominant group (PMVs) knows that it experiences life differently than the subdominant (FIW) group. However, while the dominant group knows there is a difference, it is only the subdominant that knows what that difference is. And even then the subdominant group finds it difficult to come up with a vocabulary that helps them articulate the specifics of that difference. It becomes evident here that MGT is providing the framework from within which to evaluate the interactions between FIWs and PMVs. Dominant and subdominant groups do have differing life experiences, and this indeed affects communication.

Tenet #2 - Muting

> *The dominant group's life experiences differ from the subdominant group's life experiences, which leads to the muting of the subdominant group.*

According to MGT the dominant group is privileged, and it is clear that whether or not they are comfortable with the idea, within the prison context the PMVs are a more dominant group than the FIWs. Therefore, because much of the FIW life experience is different and thus not relevant to PMVs, FIWs are often muted. Remember, muting in MGT does not mean that verbalization is not physically possible; it means that voice is silenced, or if heard at all, is disregarded as irrelevant.

When I compared FIWs and PMVs answers to the interview question, "Spiritually speaking, what are the most difficult things to communicate about with prison ministry volunteers/prisoners," FIWs identify difficulties in communicating with PMVs much more frequently than PMVs do in communicating with FIWs. Two-thirds of FIWs answered affirmatively about difficulties compared to less than half of the PMVs. This same trend is repeated in responses to the question "Have you noticed any differences between how prisoners and prison ministry volunteers talk about church?" Eighty percent of the FIWs perceived a difference compared to only forty-two percent of PMVs.

Such responses are entirely consistent with what MGT tells us to expect if PMVs are the dominant group. The dominance of the PMVs over the FIWs is in no way diminished because the PMVs are not, within the prison context, dominant over the correctional staff or chaplains. This reality, that the volunteers have less power than the prison staff, in no way changes the fact that PMVs still have more power than the prisoners. The Chaplain affirms that this power dynamic is important. When I asked the Chaplain "What questions about communication between prisoners at CIW and prison ministry volunteers have I forgotten to ask?" her reply was an emphatic assertion that the PMVs needed to know that they are coming into the prison with a "privileged perspective."

So what does it mean that the PMVs have a privileged perspective? This is a loaded term, which needs some unpacking. First, there is the privilege of demographics, whether the group being discussed is predominantly made up of the culture's majority culture persons or minority culture persons. The second is the privilege of language and of possessing the power to create and dictate what language usage is acceptable.

Privilege of Demographics

In Chapter 3, as I introduced you to my friends, there was a difference in the ethnic composition of the two groups. The difference between the ethnic diversity of the FIW group and the disproportionately large percentage of Caucasians in the PMV group, while significant, is not a weakness of my research method but is actually fairly representative. On one hand, given the small subject sample, the ethnic diversity of my FIW friends reasonably reflects the strong minority presence of the prisoner population at CIW. On the other hand, there are in fact a disproportionate number of Caucasian PMVs at CIW.

During her interview, Marsha (FIW) addresses one reason for this imbalance. She strongly asserts that current institutional clearance policies for people applying for permission to enter CIW are at play. The clearance approval process, which entails application forms to be filled out and background checks performed, favors, in Marsha's words, "upper class, more affluent whites" who do not have preexisting knowledge of prison or relationships with prisoners. The process effectively excludes many African-Americans who, by reason of being incarcerated at a higher rate than whites, have more prior experience with prison. Point in fact, only two PMVs had been themselves incarcerated in the past, the two African-American men. Further, and also consistent with dominant group privilege as stated in MGT, white majority culture volunteers are more easily able to navigate the bureaucratic channels necessary to achieve entry into CIW as PMVs than minority group members are. After all, majority group PMVs speak the language of the dominant group.

One additional factor of privilege and dominance in communication between PMVs and the women prisoners at CIW is that at least a percentage (in this study 25%) of PMVs are male. MGT is most often cited in terms of gender communication, with the dominant group identified as male and the subdominant group identified as female. Thus, the fact that the PMV group contains some men strengthens the position that the PMVs are the dominant group in MGT terms. It is particularly telling that the fifty-eight percent of PMVs who had stories about prisoners misunderstanding them included all five of the men.

Privilege of Language

The dominant group that creates language in the prison is the California Department of Corrections and Rehabilitation (CDCR), the same dominant entity that labels prisoners "inmates." To some extent then, PMVs must learn the language of the dominant culture. Cindy likened it to business, where "every industry and business has its own lingo and you should not try to lose your business lingo when you're not with somebody who's in that business."

Janet seemed to find the language of prison a bit more of a challenge. "When you're a volunteer, you're in a different world, and it takes a while before you understand what the dictionary and the glossary of terms means. You know, it's like, 'Hmm. Okay. That's what that means?'" Thus she admits that the way prisoners use language "could be a big communication problem."

However, just because the PMVs are the group that must learn unfamiliar prison lingo does not mean that prisoners are, in this instance, dominant group members. Prisoners, too, have to learn the language of prison, since there are no native-born speakers in prison. Everyone comes to prison from somewhere else. Add to this that the majority of prisoners come from marginalized populations, whether due to race, ethnicity, socio-economic status, gender identification, or other factors, and therefore have never been members of the dominant group.[87] While both PMVs and prisoners are thus subdominant groups that must learn to use the language of CDCR, in reality, prisoners are simply subdominant to both the CDCR and to the PMVs simultaneously.

PMVs are especially privileged in terms of the language about the church, which the interview question, "Have you noticed any differences between how prisoners and prison ministry volunteers talk about church?" revealed. Janet referred to prisoners who "mimic the language" of the church, which she thought they may be picking up from television. In another example, I am grateful to Jim for articulating the observation that prisoners "call anybody who's coming from the outside as prison fellowship, they call that church." This is actually a major linguistic difference; PMVs and FIWs do not share the same definition of "church." I did not realize this at first. I, like my FIW friends, make no distinction between church and any other faith-based activity. This resulted in my serious consternation with PMVs who told

---

[87] This is where my privilege exists. Although a subdominant prisoner, I was raised in dominant group culture as a white daughter of a college professor. My dominant culture background has had a vital role in allowing me to bridge between PMV and FIW vocabularies. And yet my dominant background completely fails me in trying to communicate some of the life experiences that I share with my FIW friends.

me that they could not answer the question as to differences in how PMVs and FIWs speak about church because, after all, they only came in to provide Bible studies and did not provide church services. In prison we had presumed that any activity at CIW that involved a PMV was automatically "church."

In yet another example, Ben related an entire story that had, in other settings and with other people, been used successfully to communicate dramatically what Jesus' incarnation means. The story was about God taking you to visit another world, which was inhabited only by dogs, and then asking you to love them, become like them, and suffer at their hands. The punch line went: "But God said, there's one more thing. I'm going to resurrect you after they kill you, but you need to know that when I do, you're going to be a dog for the rest of eternity. That's what Jesus did for us." Ben recognized that there had been an obvious communication issue due to the reaction of a woman prisoner who angrily walked out of the room. He attributed her reaction to her being upset that Jesus was being compared to a dog. This encounter had bothered Ben, but he told me that he was committed to continuing to use the story because it had been so useful in other settings.

The possibility that the prisoner was interpreting the story as comparing her to a dog never occurred to him. Yet, as in insider, I understood immediately that this is what had happened. Inside prison, the term "bitch" is much more frequently used to refer to a woman than it is to a female dog, so women prisoners are sensitized to such a comparison. Ben's story triggered a particularly painful memory of my own. This memory was of a Correctional Counselor[88] who was preparing my evaluation prior to a parole board hearing. This staff confronted me with the words, voiced with scorn and acid, "Even a dog knows how to protect its young. What's your explanation for letting your child die?" I was devastated. However, it was vital that I still maintained my composure, through my tears, as I tried to communicate the unexplainable. He approved my answer, wrote a positive report, and I am sure forgot the exchange decades ago. I still carry the wounds.

So, in terms of dominant group privilege, MGT is both framework and theoretical construct. MGT explains power dynamics and process of dominant group language privilege that sheds light on communication issues between FIWs and PMVs. And here again, MGT is being applied beyond the boundaries of gender communication to explain, in this instance, the levels of dominance and subdominance between CDCR, PMVs and FIWs. Power is privilege, and privilege is power. This is just as true in communication dynamics at CIW as in any other milieu.

Tenet #3 – Consequences

> *Subdominant group members must either learn to use the dominant group language or suffer the loss of societal benefits.*

Muting is not passive. Muting is something that is done to someone, specifically to the subdominant group members. Subdominant group language issues are both the cause of and the result of that muting. I discovered that communication gaps between FIWs and PMVs

---

[88] A Correctional Counselor I, (CCI) is a custody staff person, at the hierarchical level of a Sergeant, whose duties include preparing parole board hearing reports evaluating a prisoner's "institutional adjustment," as in disciplinary history, work history, etc.

are more directly revealed within the interview. However, the muting for FIWs is often less obvious, revealed by what is not said. Especially in the micro difference power dynamic that occurs between FIWs and PMVs, muting is frequently subtle. Therefore, evidence of muting often must be teased out by looking within the interview transcripts for what FIWs and PMVs are revealing indirectly.

Muting

Prison mutes. In the massive power difference between CDCR and prisoners, muting is not a covert and subtle activity. For example, universally known to prisoners and virtually unknown to the general public is that the media is restricted from interviewing prisoners without the explicit permission of prison administration and CDCR; this permission is not often granted. In particular, the media is not allowed to interview just one specific prisoner.

In a personal example, the Montel Williams Show became interested in my story in 2006. At that time, I had been granted parole for the seventh time, and was awaiting a decision by then Governor Arnold Schwarzenegger. However, the producers were not able to get permission to interview me. So instead, the producers asked permission to interview some of the prisoners involved with Chaffey Community College's pilot Associate Degree program, for which I was one of the facilitator-tutors. Permission was granted. The producers arranged, and Montel Williams conducted, interviews of several Chaffey prisoner-tutors, some Chaffey prisoner-students, some of the Chaffey faculty, and some custody staff about the program. When it was my turn to be interviewed, Montel took considerably more time with me, delving into the circumstances of my life and crime in addition to my role as a

Chaffey prisoner-tutor. When the segment aired, the entire hour show was focused on me. I was informed later that the Warden and CDCR higher ups were furious; however their anger was focused on the producer. After all, I was just a powerless prisoner without voice. Incidentally, while generating much public support for my release, this show did not move the Governor. My parole was again reversed.

In other examples of overt muting, prisoner phone calls are universally monitored. There is always a threat of punishment or withheld privileges for anything deemed "inappropriate" communication. In the dining hall, the loudest voices are those of the Correctional Officers (COs) yelling, "Quiet! You're here to eat, not talk!" In the halls of the prison clinic, again the COs loudly demand, "No talking! It's too loud in here!" with the implication of disciplinary action and loss of medical services for noncompliance.

In addition to this gross muting, my friends confirmed my experiences that prisoners are muted in various manners within the prisoner/ministry volunteer relationships. The following is a representative, non-exhaustive, list of examples of ways that prisoners are thus muted.

Muting occurs when prisoners are not allowed to express worship in exuberance.

PMVs admit that they perceive the prisoners as sometimes having too much freedom in expressing worship. Ben explained that the services are "a little bit disorganized" and "weren't done so decently and in order." However, the FIWs explicitly recognize that they have been muted.

Diane explained that when the PMVs are not open to receive people "who show an outward array" of worship that the "women are stigmatized." Diane specifically referred to Rhoda, an FIW we both know, who was well known for her ecstatic and uninhibited expressions of being "touched by the Spirit," in which she would sing, dance, and pray in tongues. Diane and I both smiled fondly at the memories of Rhoda's joyful exuberance. But many PMVs, especially those not from a Pentecostal background, found her behavior inappropriate. She was frequently chastised, asked to be quiet, or even asked to leave the service if she could not control herself. PMVs often saw Rhoda as a problem; FIWs know that she is just a sister who has her own style of "coming to Jesus."

Muting occurs when PMVs take over prisoner-led groups and activities.

Diane went on to explain the process by which PMVs repeatedly took over events. Prisoners would have an idea for an event, such as a Christian retreat or concert, to which, as it was being organized, they would invite PMVs to join as guests. Then those PMVs "all of a sudden didn't like the way the programs were done, didn't like the way we set up this, didn't like, didn't like." What started out as a prisoner-led event, would be taken over and turned into something unrecognizable to the prisoners. Instead of a platform for prisoners to preach and teach each other and share with guests, the PMV "guests" would take over, eliminating the prisoners from the speaker list, replacing them with PMVs. Thus, a double muting, muting by taking over the planning of the event, but also by preventing prisoners from using their voices during the event. As Diane says, "it always happened."

This tendency for PMVs to take over prisoner-led activities was noticed even by some of the PMVs. Judy described behavior she observed from one of her team members. While they were conducting a Bible study in the prison, a team member took over what Judy called an "inmate-led group." And when the prisoner who had been assigned to lead the group "tried to voice" that she had been asked to lead the group, the volunteer refused to listen and insisted on taking charge. Judy admitted that the situation "was not good. I apologized to the inmate and said it was totally our mistake. Uh, but I wasn't able to fix it." Wounds, especially those that result from muting, can be healed, but they cannot be undone.

Muting occurs when prisoners are not recognized or empowered for leadership.

Another form of muting occurs when prisoners are not recognized as already being leaders within the prison church. One way this happens is when PMVs appoint leaders without being aware of who is already leading within the prison church. As Rosa noted, "They have preference. They only choose the person who they like. They give more attention to them."

Ruby tells about one PMV who would refer to specific prisoners as positive examples without thinking through the repercussions. "She would use her power to call out those that she knew. But what about those people that you don't call out to them? You're making them feel like they're not a person."

Diane points out that PMVs don't recognize the growth within the individual prisoner that transforms her from one who started out in need to one who has been empowered to mature. "Now you're being creative. Now you're having your own visions, your own dreams." To some PMVs, all prisoners are presumed spiritual babies, even those who came to Christ while in prison but have been growing, learning, and maturing for decades. Diane appreciates PMVs for having been instrumental in the spiritual growth process, but "now it's time for me to grow up and walk in what you all have graciously taught us over ten, fifteen years."

Muting occurs when quiet prisoners are not encouraged or pulled forward.

As subdominant group members, some prisoners have over-learned the lesson of discretion. As a PMV, Janet credited the silence of prisoners to their not being able to "say what they really think too often." But sometimes it is more than the prison environment, but the actual communication style of the PMV that enforces the silence. Gail was put off by PMVs who come off as if they "already have all the answers with God," when a "humble" style would work better. She ultimately avoided misunderstandings with PMVs by "barely" talking to them.

Jill is a quiet person who, when we were incarcerated together, was part of the prisoner ministry team of which I was Moderator. Jill simply laughed and said, "I just left dealing with [the PMVs] to you."

Muting occurs when prisoners are denied meaningful topical conversations.

The prison administration actively mutes PMVs on certain topics in a manner that filters down to additional muting of prisoners. One major example of this, as I discussed earlier in Chapter 6 is the topic of denominations. The Chaplain recounted how she specifically trains PMVs to not "proselytize." What this means to her is, "we do not go against another religion there at the prison." Therefore, she further explains, although PMVs are expected to "teach Jesus Christ," they are not allowed to say anything against the teachings of other denominations such as Latter-Day Saints or Jehovah's Witness. This effectively prevents prisoners from having any meaningful conversation with PMVs about the entire topic of denominations. The Chaplain mutes the PMVs and the PMVs mute the prisoners. The end product is paroling prisoners do not have enough information about the various denominations to go about finding a spiritual home outside prison that suits their individual worship styles and needs.

Muting occurs when PMVs make "I've got the keys" power plays.

It is often the case that PMVs are issued keys, the ultimate symbol of power to those who live behind locked doors. However, it is not those keys in themselves that create muting. It is when PMVs wield that power for the deliberate sake of silencing a prisoner that muting occurs. Lisa spoke of fellow volunteers who come in as if they have "the power" and of PMVs who are known to resolve disputes with prisoners by saying, "I have the keys and I'm in charge." Again, the issue is how, not what. I have worked with PMVs who could communicate the above in such a way that they were simply stating the obvious reality and that the bottom-line responsibility was theirs. But I have also worked with PMVs who could use the same words to convey their relish of power in a manner that is totally dehumanizing and silences any rebuttal.

In a refreshing turnabout, I recently had lunch with an FIW friend, Nina, who is now not only a PMV, but a "Brown Card" holder.

Only those PMVs with brown ID cards are allowed to escort a team of PMVs without a custody staff. Nina has the keys, and the responsibility that goes with those keys. But as a returning prisoner, she is perceived as one who has overcome muting, attained voice, and gives voice to us all.

Subdominant Language

The original transcriptions that I made of these interviews are verbatim, with uncorrected grammar, word usage, or pronunciation. Studying them in this form was extremely important to my research since MGT contends that subdominant group's life experiences are not adequately reflected in dominant group language. As the subdominant group, FIW word inventions, such as Diane's use of the word "safetiness" as a value of Christian faith, reflect this. Another example is Carol's use of the word communication, which I realized, when examining its use in context, is intended to mean something closer to community and communion. Carol is using the subdominant group language, or rather not using any language because nothing fits her experience, and yet she believes that other FIWs will understand what she means due to shared experiences. That she is correct in this presumption is evidenced by the fact that I am able to translate her actual meaning to you.

As mentioned above, in describing the language that prisoners use to communicate spiritual things, PMV Jane observed that prisoners, "tend to mimic the language, they model the language of what they're taught. The actions, or the words…that are given to them." She thinks this happens because prisoners are "sheltered from so many varieties outside." There was also some discussion by both FIWs and PMVs subjects about the differences in vocabulary between prisoners and outsiders. Maria specifically mentioned "certain lingo that you use" such as "canteen," and PMV Cindy referred to "popping doors lingo." However, there was no perception of this regarding church vocabulary. This interpretation that FIWs are mimicking the language they hear from the PMVs, and possibly from other sources such as television is entirely consistent with MGT, a clear incidence of the dominant group creating the language and the subdominant group learning and using the dominant group language, even if their experiences are not adequately or identically described by the dominant group language.

Another example of subdominant language usage revealed itself to me when a professor reading an early draft of my work noted that Kathy did not use an antecedent to the word "there." He was confused as to what she had intended to communicate. I had entirely overlooked this as an issue, because we FIWs know that "there" is always CIW. It became the central location of our life. And it is the place where we no longer are. So whether we refer to the prison as "there," as "C.I.Wonderful," as "the dark place," or "the convent," shared experience supplies the context that defines the term.

The following is a one-paragraph excerpt from Lisa's (a PMV) interview transcription. I will use this example to trace the process from muting to subdominant language usage.

> I've seen volunteers that come in as if "I've got the power. I've got the keys. I'm in control." And I remember one time, and it was within the last year, I was working with a volunteer who kinda got into a tiff with an inmate. And I thought, you've got to be kidding me. And she said, "I have the keys and I'm in charge." And I thought, you have lost your audience, (laughs) because this is not about that...But it rocked the inmate. And I was really bothered.

> And I talked with the volunteer about it and Tina [another volunteer] talked with her. And it was such an abuse of it. And I just thought, "She just got real human." But she went somewhere that I'd never seen anyone go. So, I know that it can happen.

At first glance, this is simply a case of overt muting. The dominant group volunteer used her power to silence a subdominant group prisoner. However, a closer examination of the elements of this example reveals multiple dimensions of muting. Although the antecedents are unclear in "this is not about that," Lisa, the PMV, was stating that ministry was not about power. Further, she was minimizing the importance of power dynamics. However, as Lisa observed, the prisoner was strongly affected, and the volunteer "lost her audience." Or, to use the muted response designations discussed earlier, the prisoner, in reaction to the overt muting, became angrily disengaged. This response manifested itself in two ways. First, the prisoner left the room and physically withdrew. Secondly, when Lisa talked with her later, the prisoner was not placated.

What is a little subtler here, but still clearly present, is the contrast between referring to the prisoner as "inmate" and referring to the volunteer who is asserting her power in an abusive manner as "she just got human." The painful irony is that prison teaches subdominant group members that, when we let go of restraints and act out inappropriately, we lose our humanity and are pronounced "inmates." Yet when the same kind of thing happens to a dominant group member, she is identified as acting "real human."

Another element present in this interview excerpt is that the word "control" has multiple meanings to prisoners that are lost on outsiders. Consider the following: at one point when I was in prison, a new administration had determined that the cost of prisoner hygiene supplies were being wasted and instituted a new policy whereby the supply closets were to be locked and prisoners were to request supplies from their housing officers. The room in which the officers, hygiene supplies, and control panels for locking and unlocking cell doors were located was commonly referred to as "Control." This resulted in the multi-layer prison maxim of *"The tampons are in control!"* Layer 1: Literally, you must go and ask (sometimes beg and justify your need) for the female hygiene product from the (probably male) CO sitting in the central office because *"The tampons are in Control."* Layer 2: When there is disruption on the living unit, everything is in chaos (perhaps even a medical emergency) and the CO cannot be found, to the question "Why isn't the cop in control?" the answer given is, *"Because the tampons are in control."* Layer 3: When the presence of a CO is needed, but the officer is in conference with several others in the office (usually about either union issues or the results of the latest sporting event), a safe way of making a disrespectful reference to officers is to say, *"The tampons are in control."* Layer 4: Building on the previous concept, when new rules are instituted that are punitive, irrational, and deeply hurtful, they can do whatever they want to us because *"The tampons are in CONTROL!"*

    Framing the above in terms of MGT, prisoners, as the subdominant group, have developed ways to use the dominant group language to describe concepts and situations that are outside the dominant group life experiences. Thus, this single paragraph from an interview with a PMV yielded a number of separate power dynamics.

Tenet #4 – Resistance and Change

Resistance and change are possible!

The development of MGT as a theory would be pointless if there was no resultant possibility of resistance to muting, and no possibility for change. The same could be said for this book. However, resistance and change are indeed possible.

The Muted Can Resist Being Muted

Here I am, an FIW and PhD, who resisted my own muting. I am speaking for myself, but I am also providing a voice for my silenced FIW sisters. Each FIW who participated in this study is helping give voice to all subdominant woman prisoners. Some of these FIW subjects are, in their own ways, dedicating their lives to providing voices to the muted women in prison. Diane runs a substance abuse center and teaches social workers how to listen to women coming out of prison. Julie provides voice through her singing engagements, sharing the loveliness of a voice that has come out of prison. Marsha serves on her church council as the voice of the formerly incarcerated. Rosa is doing mission work among her own people in the barrios of Tijuana, Mexico. And Eva leads the prison ministry at a large church. There are other FIWs, who for various reasons were unable to participate in this study, but who supported the concept of this study through encouragement, prayers, and fostering connections to other women who might be possible subjects. Finally, do not discount the women who are still incarcerated at CIW and other prisons, but who are finding ways to resist being muted and to have their voices heard.

The Muters Can Resist Muting

Each PMV who participated in this study has taken a step towards confronting the muting of the prisoners. Further, their very discomfort with power is evidence that many PMVs consciously do not want to dominate, do not want to use power to harm the women they are ministering to. It is my hope, and I believe theirs, that this research will provide PMVs with helpful knowledge about the mechanics of muting.

In another example, Fuller Theological Seminary and the distinguished faculty who found merit in my scholarship, and financially provided scholarships for my studies, while I was still incarcerated are actively resisting the cultural norm of muting prisoners. I am extremely grateful.

The Muted Can Change

But the first, and most important step to change is coming to the awareness that change is not only possible, but also that change is necessary. That I have learned how to make my voice be heard is proven by the fact that you are reading this book. Not so long ago in my writing career, this was not the case. My first year of doctoral studies, I was continually marked down for my writing style by my male Japanese Teaching Assistant. His comment was that I needed to write as an academic. He did not accept my argument that I was writing as a woman, the way women communicated with women. While I still maintain that what I said was true, this was not enough to convince a dominant group person to listen to me. This has therefore meant for me, in part, learning the language of the dominant group, of the academy.

The Culture Can Change

When a culture begins to value the subdominant group(s) that abides within the greater culture, the culture itself can begin to change. I write this paragraph a few days before we celebrate Martin Luther King Day and consider how much American culture has changed in the last fifty years in order to recognize the value of our African American brothers and sisters, and to begin to hear their voices. I am not saying that I think African Americans yet have full voice; they clearly do not. Neither do women, or children at risk, or the homeless, or the poor, or any other of the subdominant groups that urban mission targets. However, culture can, and should, change, especially as dominant groups come to realize their oppression of subdominant groups.

Tenet #5 – Microcultural Differences; a Mechanism for Change

> *Microcultural power differences exist and are vital in providing a mechanism for resistance and change.*

While scholars suggested of MGT dynamics that resistance and change are actually possible, they provided no mechanism for promoting such. How do you fight City Hall? How does the subdominant group make the dominant group decide that change, that learning to listen, that resisting the dynamics that result in muting, is in its best interest? How do we make muting a relevant issue to the dominant? But if dominance is a fixed trait and if a powerful white man is always a powerful white man, then the ability to do so is nebulous. What is needed is a way to allow the dominant to realize that they, too, have been subdominant and muted at some time.

This is where my advancement of MGT makes its biggest contribution; this study proved that MGT dynamics exist even with micro power differential between dominant and subdominant group, even between FIWs and PMVs. Therefore, I argue that it is certain that even those who are most dominant have at some time experienced being subdominant and muted. In the old MGT paradigm where dominant meant male, or white, or some other designation that was permanent and fixed, the dominant group member would almost never experience being subdominant. However, in my expanded MGT paradigm, even a very successful dominant white male can relate to having been a child who was subdominant to parents, or a student who was subdominant to his professor, and thereby muted. This then creates opportunities to help the dominant group members gain the empathy and understanding they need to develop the willingness to resist and change.

As an example, youth are subdominant to adults. Further, teenagers always have a culture that is different than the adults, because they work so hard to develop exactly that in their struggles to create a distinct self-identity! Therefore, youth develop their own language and have their own life experiences that adults do not generally appreciate or respect.

"No, you will not play that awful music on the radio in MY car!" the parent exclaims to the disgust of the teenager. Whether the dominant group members identify with the adult parent who is trying to improve a relationship with a teenager or remembers those experiences as that teenager, either way there exists a reason to think that MGT might be personally valuable. To date, every powerful white man to whom I have introduced MGT and muting, using this example, has gotten the point that it is not fun to be muted and that muting is not beneficial to effective communication. Thus, the reality that MGT dynamics are present even in micro power differentials provides a mechanism for motivating the powerful, the dominant, to change.

Powerful dominant group people who do not understand subdominant group muting, do not suffer the loss of societal benefits and therefore have no ready motivation to change their behaviors. Some might try, due to a vague understanding that other people should not be silenced, but have no ready mechanism for changing their behavior. Still others have a sincere desire to communicate with others who are less powerful, and especially to communicate the gospel message to those with recognized differences in life experiences, but do not know how to bridge the gaps.

This has been a second look at how the five tenets of MGT have each played out between the FIWs and PMVs. Now I will examine MGT as a whole, and how this study of dynamics between micro power difference groups informs MGT.

Developments in Muted Group Theory

There are three main areas in which this study helps to develop MGT as a theory, each of which will be discussed in turn. The first area, which I will refer to as reflexivity, has to do with the double-blind nature of the relationship between PMVs and FIWs. The second, the relevance of micro-level power differences, emerges from the position of PMVs as simultaneously subdominant to CDCR and dominant to prisoners. The third applies MGT in a new way to help explain a major weakness and drawback of Donald McGavran's once very popular Homogeneous Unit Principle (HUP).[89]

Reflexivity

The dynamics that exist between dominant and subdominant groups is unique in this study because the subdominant group lacks knowledge of the dominant group as well as the other way around. Thus, MGT is at work in two directions in this study; there is a reflexive blindness.

I almost lost the following data point due to an initial overenthusiastic scrupulousness about not putting words in the mouths of my FIW friends. But in rereading Isazi-Diaz's comments, cited earlier regarding the difference between using and abusing subjects when the researcher is both an insider and an outsider, I realized that I indeed have something to offer this discussion as an insider of the FIW group.[90] During post-interview, I usually shared with my friends some of my personal experiences and observations that put me on this research path. It is only in the last few interviews, where I left the recorder on after the formal interview was over, that I captured some of this. The following are two FIW reactions to my perspective on why I did not have a real idea of what constituted a good church outside of CIW:

> Me.   Well, that's the other thing I've been trying to explain to people is that, those of us who come to the Lord on the inside, all we really know about church is we don't know what a good one is, 'cause if we'd been in a good one, we wouldn't have come in, right?

---

[89] Donald A. McGavran, *Understanding Church Growth*, 3rd Ed (Grand Rapids, MI: Wm. B. Eerdmans Publishing Co, 1990), 163.

[90] Isasi-Diaz, *La Lucha Continues*, 5.

> Clara. Say that! Say that!
>
> Me.   Does this resonate with you at all...
> Alice. Right. Definitely. That's true. Because I think, like you said, a lot of us attend services in there, and a lot of people that are new in Christ haven't attended any type of church, so they really don't have anything to compare it to. So, they compare it to what they know, which is the services at CIW. And then they get out and it's like the air is let of their balloon because they attend a church and they don't feel that community.

In these instances, the subdominant group has no better understanding of the dominant group experience than the dominant group has of the subdominant. The PMVs do not understand FIW experiences in prison, and the prisoners do not understand PMV experiences of church on the outside. While it is the subdominant prisoner group that is hindered from making adequate preparation for parole by not comprehending the realities of the church in the community, the PMVs simultaneously lose the opportunity to experience church in a context that is more intense, communal, and accepting than what the churches outside prison usually offer. In this new application of the theory, MGT explains the communication dynamics in both directions.

Micro-Level Power Differences and Communication

PMVs often do not realize how great the gap that is caused simply by their non-prisoner status. For the most part, PMVs can be considered simply as local missionaries, entering into the foreign culture of prison. The degree of muting of prisoners in context with PMVs is lost even on the prisoners. While PMVs do mute prisoners who thereby suffer loss, the immediate significance of this muting to the prisoners diminishes exponentially in comparison to the overt muting of the macro-level power dynamic of CDCR. A prisoner talking with a PMV has significantly fewer constraints, and is so much closer to equal power dynamic, that the micro-level dynamic is frequently overlooked, and deemed unimportant, even by the prisoner.

This is why some, both FIWs and PMVs, deny the existence of any communication gap. Some PMVs believe that they have had exceptional experiences that bridge this gap. For two male PMVs, it was that they themselves had experienced incarceration. For another PMV, it was her son who was incarcerated. What these people are missing is an awareness of the magnitude of difference between the experiences of incarcerated men and those of incarcerated women. As I often lead with when I am speaking to groups about incarceration, "When men come together in prisons they form gangs. When women come together in prisons they form families." So because these PMVs are more familiar with the practices and language of CDCR, they believe this helps to bridge the gap. And sometimes it does help. However, they then tend to discount how different the life experiences of incarcerated women are from what men experience. They do not realize that there is a new, and different language spoken here.

For another PMV, it was her fight with cancer that she believed helped her to understand and connect with the prisoners at CIW. And yet another cited growing up in an abusive alcoholic environment. Again, these experiences do help in bridging some gaps. But they are not enough to bridge all the gaps. Because the PMVs use language without any problem, because the communication gaps appear small, they presume that their small bridges are adequate to span these gaps. The

PMVs believe they are speaking the same language as the prisoners and that they are communicating effectively.

One example of this is the case discussed in Chapter 4 regarding FIWs visiting PMV churches. Although I had personally attended their church, only two of five PMVs reported that yes, a woman she had ministered to in prison subsequently visited her church. One cause for this response may have been the wording of my question, "Have any women you ministered to in prison subsequently visited your church?" While incarcerated at CIW, I was an In-House Ministry Team Moderator who coordinated the services in the psychiatric unit and assisted the PMVs. Thus, it is possible that these PMV friends overlooked my visit to their church because they did not perceive me as being someone they actually ministered to. This in itself is a perception gap. I assure you, I considered them as powerful outsiders who were teaching us about the word of God and how to experience church!

MGT allows me to account for muting on both macro and micro-levels. This is important because, while women prisoners are muted on many levels, many PMVs are similarly muted. Historically, MGT was most often used to explain the gender-based muting of women as a subdominant group to the dominant group of men. On the macro-level, while all CIW prisoners are women, many of the PMVs are also women who have thus also experienced being muted. However, one of the main points of this book is that it is an improper understanding of MGT to limit its use to the gender dynamic. So while gender dynamics are very significant, and these dynamics are present in communications between women prisoners and PMVs, it is frequently the case that women prisoners and women PMVs share membership in various marginalized, subdominant groups based on race or ethnic group, on socio-economic status, on education, and even on gender identity. But even here, the micro power difference between FIW and PMV means that MGT power dynamics are at work shaping the communicative experience of both. This is where, I maintain, MGT is invaluable, exploring other, additional and sometimes hidden, communication power dynamics.

Muted Group Theory and the Homogeneous Unit Principle

One FIW friend, Maria shared with me her experience of visiting a Victory Outreach church. Victory Outreach is a network of churches known for welcoming former drug addicts. Her observations caused me to think more deeply about how MGT helps explain a major weakness and drawback in McGavran's Homogeneous Unit Principle (HUP).[91] HUP states "People like to become Christians without crossing racial, linguistic, or class barriers."[92] Having common characteristics makes them feel at home with each other and aware of their identity as "we" in distinction to "they."[93]

Two different FIWs named Victory Outreach as a church that is accepting and welcoming to former prisoners, exactly the kind of church that HUP says would make them most comfortable. So attending Victory Outreach might initially seem like an appropriate way for prisoners to avoid the non-acceptance that they will often experience in outside churches. However, when we look at what MGT teaches us about communication power dynamics, we see the issue caused by this approach. In a congregation that remains an enclave, prisoners do not

---

[91] McGavran, *Understanding Church Growth*, 163.
[92] Ibid.
[93] Lausann Committee for World Evangelization. 1978. *The Pasadena Consultation: Homogeneous Unit Principle: Lausanne Occasional Paper 1.* https://www.lausanne.org/content/lop/lop-1, accessed 7/11/2019.

learn dominant group language and culture. Therefore, the benefits of dominant society are not attained; full integration into the church outside prison is not possible. It is necessary for parolees and other subdominant groups to become integrated into dominant society churches, or at least churches that are of a more dominant group than ex-convicts, if they wish to experience the benefits of that society and be fully integrated into that society.

In Maria's experience, Victory Outreach "was hardcore," so much so, she explained that she "couldn't even stay." She provided some details that revealed her level of discomfort, "It was just, just the inmates, a bunch of ex-convicts, a lot of men, you know, very hardcore." She continued, "I wasn't so used to it back then, I guess," referring to how difficult it is to adjust when going from a single gender prison to the world outside. "I don't know. I just, I didn't even stay for the service. I just took one look and felt uncomfortable around that many men. And just, just like, rough men!" Yet while this Victory Outreach church may be a place where male ex-prisoners are comfortable, for Maria it was off-putting.

MGT is a powerful tool for evaluating the dynamics of power between dominant and subdominant groups. MGT explains why and how the micro-level power dynamics between prisoners and PMVs results in muting. MGT has been underutilized by limiting its use to gender communications. Its usefulness in explaining the drawbacks of McGavran's HUP underscores the value of MGT once again.

Chapter 9

GSLC Case Study

This case study is one more piece of the larger study on communication issues between women prisoners and the Prison Ministry Volunteers (PMVs) at the California Institution for Women (CIW), and how those communication issues impact the perceptions that those women prisoners have about the church outside prison.

Emerging from my research with PMVs I have noted a trend in prison ministry: a handful of people, or even one individual, get involved with prison ministry in the name of a specific church without the knowledge or support of that church body. One issue with this is that such a model offers little to help paroling prisoners to transition into the Christian community at large, nor does it help well-meaning volunteers become effective representatives of the churches in this greater Christian community.

However, there do exist some churches that participate in prison ministry from a more holistic paradigm. The following case study features one such church in Claremont, California, with its history of "lone wolf" prison and reentry ministry, and its recent efforts to recognize and accept the missional call to prisoners and parolees as an integral part of this church's identity. What follows is one church's path of transition, not as a road map, but as an illustration and inspiration.

This case study focuses on the three essential factors involved in the transformation of Good Shepherd Lutheran Church (GSLC): (1) changes in leadership, (2) the influence of formerly incarcerated women, and (3) the formation of a member-initiated interest group. Specific relevant elements will be introduced chronologically for each of these factors. This chronological account will then be followed by a discussion of the same three essential case study factors. We will look at which elements of each factor are most critical to the missional transformation of Good Shepherd Lutheran Church, why these elements are particularly significant, and then give recommendation on how to implement what we learn from this case study, especially within urban ministry contexts.

Background

As of 2010, Good Shepherd Lutheran Church (GSLC) was a small Evangelical Lutheran Church of America (ELCA) congregation. Located in Claremont, California, "The City of Trees and PhDs," GSLC celebrated its fiftieth anniversary in 2012. Due to its proximity to a large retirement community for Christians who served as pastors or missionaries, the congregation at GSLC included a significant number of retired pastors and missionaries. And due to GSLC's proximity to several theological seminaries, the congregation also included a modest number of seminary graduate students. The congregation maintained cordial relationships with St. George's Jordanian Orthodox Church as well as One Way Korean Church, both of whom rented facilities from GSLC for their services.

GSLC was already a congregation that valued outreach and mission. Ways that GSLC as a congregation connected to the local community included monthly serving of a community meal and hosting both a tutoring program for local elementary school children and a Boy Scout troop on site. GSLC had a preexisting relationship with a Norwegian couple who did missionary work with shoeless children who lived in the dump in Cairo, Egypt. This couple visited Claremont for one month each summer in order to do fundraising. Another relationship already existed with a couple from Tanzania who live half time in Claremont as members of GSLC and the other half in Africa where they have founded Providence Children's Home in Kenya.

At the beginning of this study in 2010, there were several members who were already connected in various ways to Crossroads, a six-month transitional program consisting of three houses for women paroling from prison. However, these persons were merely connected to Crossroads as individuals. For example, Sally attended Crossroads programs as a Soroptimist,[94] while Sophia was a former Crossroads board member who regularly brought food and household donations to the homes. Some years prior to 2010, one previous Crossroads resident had attended GSLC for some months, but she had moved out of the area upon completing the six-month program. Most members of the congregation were unaware or only nominally aware of the existence of Crossroads less than two miles away, or of the California Institution for Women (CIW) prison less than twenty miles away. This was in spite of the fact that in 1980 CIW was, with a population of just over nine

---

[94] Soroptimist International of the Americas, a global volunteer organization that improves the lives of women and girls through programs leading to social and economic empowerment, has about 1,300 clubs in 21 countries and territories who work to economically empower women and girls.

hundred, the largest women's prison in the world.[95] No longer even the largest women's prison in the state, CIW currently houses over two thousand women, most of them from southern California.

Leadership

When this case study began in August of 2010, GSLC was a prospering but small congregation of less than 300 persons with a history of leadership issues. Pastor Dave had been recently left a widower with three young children. His wife had been diagnosed with breast cancer during their first few months at GSLC. As a result, various members of the congregation had taken up many of the leadership tasks without a great deal of coordination or supervision. In June 2012, Pastor Dave stepped down to remarry and accept another call.

After several months, the synod bishop appointed Interim Pastor Carol, whose agenda included strengthening leadership and a strong focus on Lutheran doctrine. However, in reaction to that, a major schism occurred when the fundamentalist youth director left, taking almost all the youth, and a portion of the congregation, with him.

In summer 2013, Interim Pastor Carol then stepped down, and Interim Pastor Terry, someone who had a few years previously served the congregation as a beloved part-time youth pastor, was appointed. Pastor Terry was a nonthreatening, nonchallenging, community-building peacemaker, whose priority was to bring peace and healing within the congregation while facilitating the call process for a new pastor.

After a long call process, Pastor Lara was ultimately offered the position, due in part to her interest in outreach and social justice. Pastor

---

[95] Barbara A. Owen, *In The Mix*, Albany, NY: SUNY Press, 1998.

Lara was already involved with the operation of the nearby Central City Lutheran Mission and its programs for men who are homeless, HIV positive, and/or recently released from prison, as well as for families facing food insecurity. A member of the call committee reported, "She will be behind everything you want to do! But she'll make you do the work."

One of Pastor Lara's first priorities was to help the congregation formulate a new vision statement: Our call is to love God, family, and neighbor through prayer, teaching, and action. On her part, Pastor Lara serves in a leadership position on the local interfaith council on an ongoing basis.

Influence of Former Prisoners on Good Shepherd Lutheran Church

A number of former prisoners have interacted with and influenced GSLC in the time span of this study. Although I was not the first formerly incarcerated woman (FIW) to attend GSLC, this account begins with GSLC's introduction to me, Linda. Admittedly, I do not fit the stereotype of a former prisoner. However, and just as importantly, I want to emphasize that I am not entirely atypical of women prisoners paroling from CIW.

Linda

In August of 2010, I walked to GSLC from Crossroads transitional home. I introduced myself to a man standing outside who seemed to be greeting people, saying to him, "Hello. I just got out of prison two weeks ago, and I'm looking for a home church." He responded by extending his arms and saying, "Welcome home." I had, by the grace of God, approached the president of the congregation, Neal.

Neal immediately introduced me to the leader of the new, intensive, small group adult Bible study that was being inaugurated that day.

I became a faithful attendant of both the liturgical second service and member of the mid-morning Bible study on Sundays. As other members heard my testimony and learned about the service Crossroads provided to paroling women, they began to donate to Crossroads leftover food items from church events on a regular basis. By May of 2011 I completed membership classes with Pastor Dave and was welcomed as a formal member of GSLC.

Pastor Dave asked me to give the sermon while he was on vacation, encouraging me to draw upon my experiences with preaching within the prison in order to edify GSLC. After all, I had served as lay pastor for the prison psychiatric unit for 27 of my 30 years of incarceration at CIW. While in prison I had earned a BS in Psychology from the University of La Verne via their extension program, which I immediately followed by working in the prison Mental Health Department as a peer counselor. I had also earned Fuller Theological Seminary's Certificate of Christian Study. This consisted of six master's level classes completed through distance learning. I then became a tutor/facilitator for the Chaffey Community College Associate of Arts degree program within the prison. When paroled in 2010, I was hired by Chaffey to tutor at their Rancho Cucamonga campus and had almost completed Fuller's MA Theology degree program.

Then, during the 2012 annual congregational meeting, I was elected to the twelve-member church council. I was also asked to help fill the gap until an interim pastor arrived by presiding over all but communion (I was not yet ordained) in several services. At this time, I had to explicitly explain to the congregation that my conditions of parole constrained me from having direct contact with children. As mentioned earlier, the violent man I was living with beat my two-year old daughter to death. In 1980, without the use of battered women syndrome as a mitigating circumstance, I was declared an accomplice, convicted of second-degree murder, and sentenced to a fifteen-year-to-life term in prison and subsequent five-year parole term. Hence someone else would be delivering the children's message that I had prepared. During this period I was also invited to give my personal testimony at an evening potluck event hosted by the Community Concerns Committee intended to educate and involve the congregation in community service.

As a seminary course requirement in 2013, I completed a study on GSLC's setting and context with recommendations for ministry. I presented the findings at several venues: to the interim pastor, to Community Concerns Committee, to Council, and ultimately to Pastor Lara when she was called. This is when it was first pointed out to the church that God had a purpose in locating this congregation less than two miles from Crossroads, and less than twenty miles from CIW and two additional prisons for men. One suggestion I made at this time was to find ways to reach out to local prison and parolee populations.

On one occasion, a young man, obviously struggling with schizophrenia and homelessness, entered GSLC during service and sat alone in the front row. I left my customary seat and sat next to him. When he showed interest in taking communion, I held his hand as we walked up to the altar together. After service, I invited him to help serve the baked goods I had brought for coffee fellowship. Later, several members of the congregation explained that they wanted to welcome the young man, but simply didn't know how to respond to him.

Pastor Lara and family chose to celebrate 2016 Thanksgiving at my home with my family and the family of another formerly incarcerated woman. I now post invitations in the GSLC Sunday bulletin and monthly newsletter inviting the entire congregation to my home to celebrate my annual anniversary of release from prison Freedom Party as well as my annual Christmas party. Additional GSLC social events sponsored by the Fellowship Committee are also held at my home.

Gloria

In spring of 2015, Gloria, the founder of the Action Committee for Women in Prison (ACWIP) – a program that provides Christmas gift bags for women at CIW – needed a new host church location. Gloria is an exonerated prisoner; not all FIWs and prisoners are actually criminals. Gloria was originally a death penalty case, reduced to a twenty-five-to-life sentence. After seventeen years of incarceration she was exonerated, summarily released, and the District Attorney who had knowingly prosecuted her for a crime she had not committed was convicted of malfeasance. It is ironic that a Pasadena mega-church could no longer serve as host since the two actual members of that church who were active in the program had passed away. I introduced Gloria to the GSLC council, who voted to host the prison Christmas project on a trial basis.

Packing gift bags became one of the GSLC "God's Work, Our Hands" day service projects. Five thousand gift bags were prepared and delivered to CIW and to LA County Women's Jail. Due to the success and the support of GSLC, ACWIP expanded to include Mother's Day gift bags for the women at CIW. In December 2016, another five thousand Christmas gift bags were packed and delivered to CIW and to

Los Angeles County Women's Jail. GSLC has become the permanent host of this program, and donation collection is an ongoing, all year process.

Brenda

In early 2012, I was given permission to set up a table and ask for support letters to the governor in favor of granting a compassionate release to a friend of Gloria's and mine. Brenda was a domestic abuse survivor convicted of killing her abuser, and she was now suffering from fourth stage lung cancer after serving a quarter century at CIW. In spite of the letters from the GSLC congregation, the compassionate release was denied. However, in June of 2013 Brenda was granted parole and released.

Brenda, who had been residing in Gloria's house since she had paroled, succumbed to lung cancer in February 2017. Gloria called me, crying, because the ultimate indignity was that there were no resources with which to inter Brenda, who was therefore to be given a pauper's burial. Upon relaying this news to Pastor Lara, I was invited to notify GSLC council and the Social Justice Task Force (SJTF) of the situation. Enough donations followed that Gloria was able to give Brenda a proper interment and send Brenda's ashes to her daughter who lived out of state.

Nova

Prior to the 2015 Christmas project bag-packing event, I had received permission from Pastor Lara to ask GSLC members working at that event to write letters to the parole board on behalf of my friend, and former CIW in-house ministry partner, for Nova's release. I provided a fact sheet about Nova, her case, her adjustment in prison, and a sample letter with pointers for what would be most helpful to have included in a support letter. At this juncture an (unsuccessful) attempt was made by several members to find a job that could be promised Nova upon parole. Nova was found suitable for parole by the Board of Prison Hearings and began the obligatory five-month long wait for the hearing results to be confirmed, first by the Hearing Review Board and then by the governor. Nova wrote thank you letters to GSLC and began to create relationships via correspondence. In September of 2016, Nova paroled to Crossroads and began regularly attending GSLC services and events with my family.

By March 2017, she had graduated from the Crossroads initial six-month program to the secondary alumni program house. Although she was unable to accept the offers due to her parole requirement to abide within Los Angeles County, two different members of GSLC who lived in the adjacent city/county invited Nova to live in their homes upon transitioning out of Crossroads.

Nova then began attending membership classes at GSLC. She stated in an interview that GSLC far exceeds any expectations or hopes she had about acceptance into a church upon paroling from prison. "The church I am going to is more than I could have even expected…it's a feeling of belonging, and that's what's so very important, you know? I look forward to going there! I haven't even thought about going elsewhere." The most meaningful way to her that GSLC showed their acceptance of Nova was when she realized that, in the photo display posted on the bulletin board of a recent church event, she was included.

By January 2018, Nova was officially welcomed to GSLC as a full member. She has attained full-time employment. She has entered a residential program that allows her an additional one-year of rent-free housing while she continues her transition into society. She regularly joins a team from GSLC to assist in hosting meals at the Central City Lutheran Mission in San Bernardino. Nova has been elected to serve on the GSLC 2018-2019 Council.

Member-Initiated Interest Group

There was no pre-existing prison ministry or social justice action group at GSLC in 2010. The inception, development, and activities of the Social Justice Task Force are as follows.

Formation of the Social Justice Task Force

An initial six-week long discussion of the ELCA Social Statement on Criminal Justice had occurred at the Adult Forum in 2012. In 2016, Pastor Lara's husband, himself a Master of Divinity seminary student, began a discussion of the ELCA Social Statement on Criminal Justice, referencing two books that bring the Statement into meaningful context outside of the church. Several GSLC members who had attended these studies recognized that they were called to action in addition to words. Council was approached and voted to allow the formation of a Social Justice Task Force (SJTF), under the auspices of the Community Concerns Committee.

The first meeting of the Social Justice Task Force (SJTF) was held in 2016. It was agreed that the purpose of this task force was to explore social justice needs, to come along-side existing ministries in order to support and enhance them, and to promulgate an outward vision for GSLC. The task force was specifically not to be a ministering body or closed group. Crossroads and prison ministry was determined to be one main area of focus for this task force.

Crossroads and Prison Ministry

With the possibility of Nova paroling soon, it was determined that the SJTF would commit to making Nova a test case for learning how to come alongside women who are paroling to Crossroads. Special focus was given to determining which resources already existed, so that efforts would not be uselessly duplicated. Where there were gaps in providing needed resources, they could be filled. Representatives of the SJTF met with the Crossroads director in order to learn more about the program and how Good Shepherd could support the work that Crossroads does. By September 2016, SJTF members began regularly joining the crew of volunteers at Crossroads' monthly event to perform yard cleanup and basic maintenance of the halfway house grounds.

SJTF members also regularly volunteer at the monthly re-entry fair held by the local Parole Office. Several more letter campaigns have had, as to be expected, mixed results. Two of the long-term prisoners were denied parole while a third is now living at Crossroads.

Martina and the Church in Tijuana

Another topic discussed by the SJTF was the possibility of giving financial and spiritual support to Martina. I have, in previous chapters introduced Martina, a formerly incarcerated woman who had been my cellmate for the final thirteen years of my incarceration, but who, as an undocumented person, was deported to Mexico upon parole. Martina ministers to the homeless and destitute in Tijuana by serving burritos along with God's Word, while she and her pastor's wife also attend Bible college. Some members of the church, all of whom subsequently joined the SJTF, had been giving pocket money to me to take with me on my monthly trips to Tijuana to support Martina. A proposal was made by SJTF to Council for GSLC to support Martina. Because Martina is an individual and not a corporate entity, Community Concerns and Council decided that it was not feasible for a budget line item to be created to support Martina. However, individual contributions of money and staple food items were greatly encouraged. Community Concerns would look into obtaining large print Bibles in Spanish.

Three different members of the SJTF, including Pastor Lara, have each taken a turn in joining my husband and I on our monthly trips to Tijuana to see and support Martina.

Pastor Nora

Pastor Nora is the coordinator of a monthly re-entry fair where recently paroled persons are invited to connect with various local groups that provide resources and assistance. Pastor Nora addressed the newly formed SJTF via Skype, and as a result, several SJTF members joined me in volunteering at Pastor Nora's local Reentry Fair.

Pastor Nora extended an invitation to join with her urban mission group and the Catholic Archdiocese in hosting restorative justice programs within the local prisons. Two members of the SJTF completed this training in 2017, and plans for bringing Restorative Justice classes to GSLC are ongoing.

Pastor Nora also coordinates an Inside/Outside Art Show for currently and formerly incarcerated persons from local prisons. A percentage of the proceeds of sales go towards buying art supplies for prisons. A second portion of the proceeds are donated by the prison artists towards the Pomona Valley Reentry Coalition. The remainder goes to the prisoner or former prisoner artist.

At the 2016 annual GSLC "alternative Christmas gift" fair, one table was dedicated to the Inside/Outside art show. A second table was dedicated to selling Martina's hand-made beaded jewelry. One SJTF member proposed and facilitated approval for the October 2017 Inside/Outside Art Show to have a follow-up venue at a local art association gallery located in a major local shopping mall. Pastor Nora has also accompanied my husband and me on one of our monthly visits to Tijuana to meet Martina.

Educational Events

The SJTF began presenting an annual educational event, consisting of four consecutive Sunday afternoon presentations on a specific topic. The topic for 2017 was "Understanding our Muslim Neighbors," and members of the local mosque were invited to participate in the presentations. In 2018, a previously quiet member of the GSLC congregation, Kay, revealed that she was a County Sheriff who headed the anti-trafficking taskforce. She then became an active member of the SJTF, and helped coordinate presentations on this topic. This development is particularly significant because, as a Sheriff, Kay visits some of the victims of trafficking who have ended up incarcerated at CIW.

In 2019, the SJTF topic of the year, very much influenced by this research project, was providing voice to our marginalized neighbors. In addition to a full session on Muted Group Theory, other sessions focused on those marginalized due to gender identity, race and ethnicity, citizenship status, and previous incarcerations. Leaders at GSLC are making deliberate decisions to respect and listen to the voices of the less dominant groups. If gaps are not immediately and totally bridged, there is an effort to ensure that the gaps are being named and acknowledged.

GSLC Case Study Analysis and Application

So, what does this case study teach about how to mobilize an entire congregation to embrace a missionary vision towards prison ministry and re-entry care of former prisoners? And how does MGT inform this process? It boils down to the three elements: of leadership, of contact with prisoners and former prisoners, and of a member-initiated interest group. Although these are addressed separately for the sake of the case study, they are actually reflexive and intertwined.

Change of leadership is always a time of turmoil. In this instance, change of leadership also provided opportunity for a change of direction or focus. At GSLC, since the new leader was a woman (in an interracial marriage), she had more personal experience of being a subdominant group member. She was therefore more deliberate in giving focus to hearing the voices of the subdominant group members both in her church and in her community.

However, it is not necessary to hire a new pastor in order to move a church towards a prison mission vision. Approaching from the angle of promoting internal change within the pastor and church leadership could possibly be even more effective at helping the entire congregation embrace prison mission as its calling.

At GSLC, the member-initiated SJTF was a later development influenced by both the personal relationships formed with prisoners and former prisoners and by a leadership that was conducive to such a development. I suspect that the member-initiated interest group is more critical to the promulgation of involvement by the congregation as a whole than it is to initiation of the missional focus. Prison ministry teams cannot function effectively as isolated and unrecognized subsets of the congregation. In addition to a lack of accountability and training that results from such situations, individual "lone wolf" ministers are at higher risk of remaining unaware of programs within the community. They are thus at risk of pouring energy into ineffective efforts that are already paralleled within the community.

Prison ministry is not a unidirectional ministry. Those ministering in prison must bring the prison back to the church if that church is to develop a missional attitude towards the prison and prisoners. The entire church must be moved, through inspiration and education, to accept and welcome a parolee. Until an entire church is moved to identify accepting and walking alongside parolees as part of its missional identity, there will only be "lone wolf" ministries. Churches will be greatly hindered in ministering to released prisoners and accepting them in their midst, if their members have not been helped to surmount their own fears, prejudices, and traumas related to crime and criminals.[96]

Nova and I are fully integrated members of GSLC. Liturgical prayers for the people currently include prayers for the prisoners and former prisoners. Prison ministry has come to be seen, not as something that a few members are loosely involved in, but as part of the missional calling of Good Shepherd Lutheran Church. Prison ministry is not the only missional calling of this Christian community. GSLC is active in various ministries such as feeding the hungry, interfaith dialogue and

---

[96] Linda Barkman, "Towards a Missional Theology of Prison Ministry" *International Journal of Pentecostal Missiology,"* (2017). In this article I explain the need for, and mechanics of, developing contextual theologies of prison ministry for missional churches.

relationship building, and intergenerational care that includes youth and elderly. However, these, along with the Prison Ministry, are all understood to be aspects of God's calling upon the entire congregation within its context.

As the research results of the greater project here show, landing in a church that is hospitable and accepting of a formerly incarcerated person is not the universal experience. Why did I not experience muting at GSLC? The fact is, I did experience muting, although I was not able to identify it as such initially. I did not understand the liturgical language used by the GSLC members. I did not have any idea of what a "narthex" was, or even for that matter, what a "Lutheran" was. I felt hurt and silenced when the liturgical Prayers of the People remembered victims of crimes and those unfairly imprisoned but excluded the "guilty prisoners." I realize that others often consider me to be a victim who was unfairly convicted and incarcerated. I know there is some truth in this. Nevertheless, given what I consider the reasonable responsibilities of a mother, I identify myself as a guilty criminal. My heart ached for my precious and redeemed sisters inside who were excluded from these prayers.

What happened at GSLC, over time, is that I exposed the most powerful and influential members of the dominant group (Pastor, Council, Committee leaders) to the life experiences of the subdominant group (women prisoners) in a way that bridged some of the communication gaps. At the very least, the dominant group became aware that a gap existed. Thus, at the very inception of the SJTF, I was more appointed than invited to join with the explanation that I was needed precisely to help bridge the communication gap that the other members now understood existed.

Chapter 10

Muted Group Theory and Urban Mission

The title of this book has declared its intention to inform urban mission as a field about Muted Group Theory. However, so far, this book has concentrated on prison, and the applications of MGT to prison ministry. Now, in this chapter, I will address some of the major topics within missiology in general, and urban mission in particular, realizing that there is much crossover between the two. I will suggest ways in which MGT could be applied within each of these fields and contexts to further communication, and especially communication of the gospel message. I invite you to imagine how MGT will inform and assist you in your own areas of interest.

Applying MGT in Missiology

As a guiding theoretical framework for the case study, MGT has proven to be an invaluable tool for examining the dynamics of communication between FIWs and PMVs. MGT is no longer limited in use to explaining the types of macro power level dynamics that occur between the genders. Additionally, and most importantly, since MGT effectively describes power dynamics between dominant and subdominant groups with micro power differences, MGT provides a mechanism for promoting resistance and change. This is why I believe that MGT is an important addition to every missiologist's theoretical toolkit.

To date, the only literature I have seen in which MGT is being used as a missiological tool is that which I have written. Many persons who work in the field of missiology are aware of the dynamic between the powerful and the marginalized but do not have a clear theoretical framework for articulating this awareness. I argue that MGT is a tool that is admirably suited to exploring the subtle and overlapping dominance issues that occur within a variety of missiological disciplines. In any context where power and dominance dynamics exist (are there any where they do not?), MGT provides theoretical framework for explaining not only how these dynamics function, but also the implications of these dynamics for the marginalized and subdominant peoples.

It is also very important to keep in mind that it is not only the most dominant group in a specific culture that mutes. Again, MGT explains the process by which any group that is more dominant may be muting any group that is slightly less dominant. Missiologists must therefore specifically look for the occurrence of muting in terms of both mega level dominance differences and micro-level dominance differences. Some dominant and subdominant group-forming dichotomies are universal, such as the dominance of the rich over the poor. Others are obvious within particular cultures, such as those that exist within caste systems or within gender- and race-related power inequalities. However, not all dominance issues are universal, and not all of them are obvious. Often there are subtle, hidden power differentials and dynamics that, nevertheless, are impacting communication.

Missionaries and missiologists are not necessarily primarily dominant group members. Since it explains power dynamics between groups with small power differences, MGT can help mission workers who find themselves "caught in the middle."[97] It is as important for the missionary to be heard by those who are dominant and more powerful as it is for the same missionary to hear and not mute those who are subdominant and less powerful.

A non-exhaustive, nonexclusive listing of missiological fields follows. I include some brief thoughts and suggestions regarding how MGT applies to each.

Foreign Missions and Intercultural Communication

To many, mission means an outreach and sharing of the gospel to those of a different country, culture, and language. However, effectively communicating the gospel message cross-culturally involves more than simply translating it into the language of the dominant group. It is also important to determine where the missionary's role is privileged in ways that create power differentials. Unrecognized power differentials lead to the muting of the target group. Where mission has accompanied colonial power, missionaries have often been imbued with more power than they imagined, or perhaps even wanted, much like some of the PMVs in my research.[98] MGT thus helps explain the

---

[97] "Muted Group Theory: Caught in the Middle" is a chapter I have written for an edited book, *Theory in Practice: Case Studies in Missiology,* by A. Sue Russell, PhD, to be released shortly by First Fruits Press.

[98] R. Daniel Shaw, "Three-Day Visitors: The Samo Response to Colonialism in Western Province, Papua New Guinea." *In Colonial New Guinea: Anthropological Perspectives*, edited by Naomi McPherson. Pittsburgh, PA: University of Pittsburgh Press, 2002.

dynamics of colonial power dynamics as well as intercultural communication.

Disaster Relief

When people respond with disaster relief, without listening to those directly affected by the disaster, the results are ineffective at best, and may even become disastrous in their own right. The most vivid example of this that comes to mind is Hurricane Maria in 2017. A deadly Category 5 hurricane that devastated Dominica, the U.S. Virgin Islands, and Puerto Rico, it is regarded as the worst natural disaster on record to affect those islands. The dominant U.S. politicians minimized the death count, and over-credited the effectiveness of relief efforts. Yet one of the seminary students in a class for which I was a Teaching Assistant, explained how deliberately the voices of the subdominant Puerto Ricans, of which he is one, were being muted. Pedro, who worked for a disaster relief organization, had personally witnessed the death and destruction that Hurricane Maria had wrought on his people and his island. However, not only were relief efforts and supplies delayed, but those on site in Puerto Rico, who were attempting to report the true magnitude of the devastation, were being silenced by the government. While the official death toll account was 64, Pedro was trying to explain that in fact hundreds, perhaps thousands had died (the revised death toll in 2019 was almost 3000).

Interfaith Dialogue

Dialogue, by definition, is bifocal communication. Ideally, both sides speak, and both sides hear. But as MGT points out, by the very nature of this being an interfaith activity, there are differing life experiences on each side of the conversation. It is important to look for power dynamics, which may fluctuate back and forth, in order to recognize where muting may be occurring, and where this muting is causing communication gaps.

Children at Risk

Children, like prisoners strangely enough, comprise a group that in itself is always a subdominant group. Children are quite simply not imbued with as much power as adults are. Add to this dynamic that some children are dominant over others, while some children are simultaneously members of several subdominant groups. It is these latter ones who present a special challenge to missiologists; children who are of low socio-economic status, of racial and ethnic minority, victims of trauma, abuse, or even war, whose voices are most easily muted. MGT explains the penalty, the loss of benefits, which is incurred by those who are muted. Thus, the most well intentioned adult who inadvertently mutes a child must be aware that the effect may be diametrically opposed to the intention.

Leadership

Leadership automatically implies a dominant position within a particular context. But leadership that is predicated on the muting of subdominant groups is problematic. MGT provides an explanation of the mechanisms and consequences of muting that could be of great value to all involved. Most leaders do not understand that they are not getting the whole picture if they are not valuing the life experiences of their subordinates, and not respecting the language used to describe these experiences.

Gender-Related Areas

Especially since the emergence of the #MeToo movement, the voice of women has grown stronger. This does not mean that women have equal voice or power in most cultures, including the U.S. This area of communication, which historically embraced MGT as its own, is still informed by it. But now, with dominant and subdominant groups understood to not be fixed and unchangeable, MGT adds a mechanism for remedy, for bridging the gender gap in communication.

Urban Mission Contexts

Urban mission focuses, generally, on those who are marginalized within our inner cities. How do we account for their voices being either unheard or un-respected? How can urban missionaries help these persons to participate fully in the benefits of the larger society? MGT may provide a key to communication that provides a key to the answers. Yet while urban mission contexts may well include prison ministry, the two are not identical. Therefore, just how MGT power dynamics manifest in the various contexts will not be identical.

In the U.S., urban mission is usually taken to mean ministry to people of color, people impacted by poverty, hip hop culture, resource-deprived inner-city neighborhoods, or all of the above; however, none of these ministries are solely tied by definition to the adjective "urban."[99] However, the meaning that I prefer springs from the Scripture from which I preached my first prison sermon: "But seek the welfare of the city where I have sent you into exile, and pray to the Lord on its behalf, for in its welfare you will find your welfare" (Jer 29:7, NRSV). At CIW,

---

[99] Brad M. Griffin. 2012. "What is Urban Ministry?" in *Fuller Youth Institute Blog.* https://fulleryouthinstitute.org/blog/what-is-urban-ministry, Accessed 7/13/19.

we took this literally. When I first arrived there, CIW had its own postal zip code, for the imaginary town named "Frontera." This euphemism, like so many others, went out of favor with the California Department of Corrections and Rehabilitation (CDCR), with resultant muting. Now CIW mail is channeled to the nearby town of Corona, CA. But there is still a sense at CIW that we are our own city. And it is in praying and working for the welfare of all that we as individuals will experience God's peace.

I have thus rather arbitrarily decided to refer to the following as more specific fields within urban mission. As above, I include some brief thoughts and suggestions regarding how MGT applies to each.

Prison Ministry and Mass Incarceration

I argued at the very beginning of this book that prison ministry is a mission area that intersects with all aspects of urban mission, especially in locations such as California where mass incarceration impacts virtually every person. As local missionaries entering into the foreign culture of prison, PMVs are dominant group members who do not share the life experiences of the prisoners. MGT explains and makes sense of the communication gaps that frustrate effective sharing of the gospel by these messengers of Christ's gospel.

Prisoners believe that PMVs are not listening to them. PMVs believe that prisoners are forming realistic perceptions about the churches outside prison. FIWs believe that the churches outside are not accepting of them. PMVs believe FIWs feel welcomed in their churches. The first step to bridging a gap is becoming aware of its existence. The second step is learning how to build a bridge. MGT helps in both of these processes.

Homelessness

Homelessness intersects with a great many other subdominant groups such as the racially and ethnically marginalized, the poor, the mentally ill, the incarcerated, and sex trafficked. MGT helps us to realize the worth of these voices, while providing a mechanism that helps the dominant group members to hear. I recently was made aware of how my city government in Pomona, CA put listening to the homeless to good use. At first, it sounded strange, that in addition to bed space and locker space in the new homeless shelter opened this year, there was a kennel. What the people who built this shelter heard when listening to people on the street, was that many homeless persons refuse to go to a shelter if it meant leaving their pets behind. Not only is a dog good company and good protection; this pet may be the one thing that connects a street person to life and love.

Community Organizing

Here again, as discussed above about missionaries in general, given the liaison focus of bringing communities and resources together, the practitioner is liable to be found "caught in the middle" between more dominant groups who mute and the muted subdominant groups. MGT is a tool that can help in bridging gaps in both directions.

Racial Reconciliation

There is an old saying that "The slave understands the master's world, but the master is ignorant of the slave's world." This is a fairly accurate restatement of what MGT says of dominant and subdominant group life experiences. And while slavery supposedly ended with the

Emancipation Proclamation, the power dynamics that result in the muting of those enslaved continues.

And More...

There are more fields and topics that could benefit from the lessons that MGT has to teach. MGT power dynamic understanding could help Chaplains who work in hospitals, where normally dominant and powerful people find themselves suddenly weak and helpless. We could gain better understanding of how dominant culture persons could refrain from muting persons with different gender identity. Anti-slavery workers, whether dealing with victims of sex trafficking or labor trafficking or other oppressed groups, can use MGT dynamics to increase the voice and ensure societal benefits to those they help. I could go on. But it is my hope that, if you have journeyed with me thus far, you now see the possibilities and are challenged to put MGT into practice within your context, whatever your context is and wherever your context may be.

A Concluding Story: Success

My friends know that one of my favorite phrases is, "I want to change the world!" However, I am not unrealistic about this desire of mine to make this world of God's creation a bit better than how I found it. I expect to change the world by simply affecting just those people that God puts in front of me, one person at a time. Such is my motivation for writing this book. I would like to close this book by showing how, using the lessons learned from MGT, resistance and change are possible. The following is a story of subdominant culture persons finding their voices, and of dominant culture persons learning to hear what those voices are trying to say. There is hidden power in Muted Group Theory dynamics that, when brought to light, can be used to give voice to the muted and marginalized.

The Social Justice Taskforce (SJTF) of Good Shepherd Lutheran Church held its third annual educational series recently. This year, the topic for our four weekly sessions was "Hearing the Voices of the Marginalized." For the first ninety-minute session, I was asked to give a presentation on Muted Group Theory. This was my opportunity to explain to my church family what my work is about. Out of the twenty or so persons who attended, three were retired male white Lutheran pastors. The remaining attendees self-identified as dominant group members. I was very gratified by how serious they were about desiring to learn how to hear the voices of others and how to ensure that they were not muting those with less power.

Here is where my great experiment began. This was my chance to apply my breakthrough thoughts about MGT micro power difference dynamics, about providing a mechanism for effecting resistance and change. This was my first opportunity to challenge dominant group people to identify a time when, as subdominant group members, they had each been muted. Admittedly, these were people who already had a heart for hearing; that is why they were attending the event. But from the questions they asked during and after my presentation, coming to understand MGT was helpful and made a difference.

Two days later, I received an email from the chairperson of the SJTF:

> The paper this morning had what I think is another example of what you were speaking of on Sunday. Governor Newsom speaking as to why he denied parole for your friend wrote, "[She] is still minimizing her actions...and she continues to lack insight into her reasons for participating." Correct me if I am wrong or off base but it sounds to me that what he is saying is that she has not acknowledged her role in the way [he] thinks it should be stated. This contradicts the findings of the parole board which said "she had taken full responsibility for her role in the [crime]." I understand that the governor does not want to be known as the one who released her but his language to justify that sure sounds like a dominant person not wanting to hear what a subdominant person is really saying.

He understands the dynamics of muting, and is beginning to look at power dynamics in communication differently.

A week later, for the second presentation, I was the host/moderator for a panel of marginalized persons. The panel consisted of three persons. The first was Ron, an African American male PhD student from a nearby seminary. The second, Lateesha, was a "multiracial but, for the sake of the panel, I'll call myself African-American" woman who had been rescued from sex trafficking ten years ago and now worked in a rescue and reentry program, reaching back to help others out of the same life. The third panel member, Carlos, was a young male refugee from Honduras who showed us the bracelet locked onto his ankle by the U.S. Immigrant and Customs Enforcement (ICE) officers while his application for asylum was being processed. As in much of this book, I have provided new names to protect the identities of my friends. In this case, Carlos was particularly concerned that ICE would not be able to identify him as a participant. ICE does not want his voice to be heard.

I was appointed by the SJTF chair to introduce our guests. "Linda, aren't you going to talk to the panel members before we start so you can introduce them?" He expected me to use my power as moderator to speak for our guests.

"No, we are here to listen to our guests. I will let them speak for themselves." I proceeded to ask each panel member to share directly with the audience whatever information they thought was most important for us to hear. This was, after all, an exercise in hearing our neighbors. I then asked only three questions of our panel members: (1) Can you share from your life an experience/example when you particularly felt marginalized and/or silenced by the majority culture; (2) Can you share from your life an experience/example when you particularly felt you were included and given a voice by the majority culture; and (3) What can you tell us in five minutes that YOU most want us to hear and understand on the topic of marginalization?

Everything these three panel members had to say was valuable, informative, and interesting. But there were a few outstanding moments that I will share here.

Regarding question number one, each member of the panel had experienced marginalization and muting. No one had difficulty coming up with examples. To the next question, however, Ron was not able to come up with a clear answer. "I can't really answer this. I can't think of a clear-cut example of me being heard and accepted by majority culture." Ron is in his fifties, has a lot of white friends, and attends seminary; yet he could not remember a time when his unique voice was clearly heard. An hour later, when the formal session was finished and people were chatting over coffee and cookies, Ron called to me. He had been in a discussion with my husband and the two of the retired white Lutheran pastors. "Linda, I now have an answer to your earlier question. I now have a clear example of being heard!"

Lateesha is an articulate speaker, who explained that trafficked women are muted not only by the dominant culture, but by the dominant pimps who beat and exploit them. During the question and answer period that followed the formal questions, I personally addressed her.

"Lateesha, I know as a woman how thirty years in prison has affected my sense of self-esteem. And I know that this is something that my incarcerated sisters struggle with. So, my question to you is, do you think you are really a human being?"

This is not a question that most dominant culture people, or even slightly less dominant people, would think to ask. If you have never experienced gross dehumanization, the answer is obvious. Of course you are human. But Lateesha's answer was totally unexpected.

"Yes! I would say ninety percent of the time I feel totally human!" She said this with pride and a huge smile, even though tears started welling in her eyes. I understood. To someone who has been totally dehumanized, healing to the point of feeling human ninety percent of the time is an incredible accomplishment. The dominant culture people in the room did not have the life experience to imagine asking the question. But they had now accepted that muting was real, that the marginalized are worthy of being listened to. And this is resulting in them becoming aware of vastly different life experiences. Gaps are being bridged.

Carlos, through our Spanish-speaking interpreter, gave gut-wrenching accounts of gang violence in Honduras, of the murder of his brother, and of threats against his mother, sisters, and daughters. His was the account of a poor but honest man forced to choose between dealing drugs and extorting money for the gangs, or leaving his home to protect his family. The interpreter had a difficult time, several times breaking into tears and unable to translate for a minute or two. What did Carlos most want us to hear? "Honduras is a beautiful land. I love my country. And I love my family. No one comes to the United States from Honduras because we want to; we come because we have to in order to survive and to protect the people we love." This is the real voice of the refugee, the voice that ICE, as a vehicle of the dominant culture, tries so hard to silence.

Thank you for reading this book, and for hearing my voice.

"Open your mouth for the mute,
For the rights of all the unfortunate."
Proverbs 31:8

Appendix

Table 1: Summary of Difficult to Explain Spiritual Topics

Of those who replied "Yes" to the question: Do you have any stories you could share today about spiritual experiences that are difficult to explain to prison ministry volunteers/prisoners?

Difficult to explain spiritual topics	FIW	%	PMV	%
Children	4	33%	1	12%
Speaking in tongues/Holy Spirit/ Deliverance	4	33%	0	0%
God working	3	25%	1	1%
Love of God	0	0%	2	25%
Material/Economic	0	0%	2	25%
No topic offered	1	8%	2	25%

Table 2: Perception of Power by PMVs

PMV Answers to the Question: Do you think you are perceived as powerful when you interact with prisoners? How does that make you feel?	
Yes	And we should be the one that have power enough to help them because they are powerless.
No	**I don't think of myself as a powerful person**
Yes	Because I have a good command of my English language and that creates a certain aura.
No	**I think they look up to me because I am helpful** and guide them and bring them tools.
No	I'm respected but **I'm not the kind of person that really tries to be powerful.**
Yes	It makes me feel good like they're empowered because **I'm just as they are.**
Yes	**I don't think of that of myself.** I have the freedom they don't have to come and go.
Yes	**I'm not comfortable.** I can be powerful if something needs to get done.
Yes	**Conflicted.** I do have power because I can go in and out of their lives.
Yes	Because of respect. They honor us.
Yes	**A little embarrassed.**
No	**I'm just like they are.**
No	**Not powerful.** But I think hopeful.
No	**It makes me feel like I'm one of them** when we sit down with them.
Yes	I know it's by God's grace that I'm able to minister to them, not proud.
Yes	They appreciate me. They respect me. I'm a source of power because I'm there to help them.
No	**Power is not something that I relate to well.** Humility is way more valuable.
Yes	Humble.
	Yes = 11 61% No = 7 39%

Table 3: Summary of Issues with Power

Do you think there is any significant issue with power when prisoners and prison ministry volunteers communicate with each other?

Of those who answered yes:	Percentage of FIWs who say:	Percentage of PMVs who say:
Volunteers have some power	100%	54%
Volunteers have all the power	70%	23%
Prisoners have some power	30%	69%
Prisoners have all the power	0%	46%
Both Volunteers and Prisoners have power	30%	30%

Table 4: Protestant Service Schedule Nov. 2016

Sun	Mon	Tue	Wed
		1 5:45P Harrison Libres en Cristo 5:45P Sap4 Prison Fellowship Pre—Release/12 Steps	**2** 12:30P-1:30P SHU Chap Woodard 2:P-3:30P Chapel Open Line- Chaplain Woodard 5:45P Chapel Steinkamp
6: 8:30A AUD—Praise Dancers 11:30A AUD—Touch of Love 8:30A-11A Old Chapel Libres en Cristo 10A-12P SCU—First Eve Free 5:45P Old Chapel—Vineyard 2P-:3:30P Old Chapel Inner Vision	**7** 5:45P - Sap4 Shoot From The Hip	**8** 5:45P Sap4 Prison Fellowship Pre-Release/12-Steps	**9** 12:30P-1:30P SHU Chaplain Woodard 2P-3:30P Chapel Open Line Chap Woodard 5:45-P Chapel Wmen Aglow
13 9A-12P Harrison—Libres en Cristo 10A-11A SCU—Aglow Prison Ministry 11:30A-Old Chapel Shoot From The Hip 5:45P Old Chapel—Prison Min. of America	**14** 5:45P Sap4 Living Waters	**15** 5:45P Harrison Libres en Cristo 5:45P Sap4 Prison Fellowship Pre-Release/12-Steps	**16** 12:30P-1:30P SCU Chap Woodard 2P-3:30P - Open Line- Chaplain Woodard 5:45P Chapel Chaplain Woodard
20 9A-12P Old Chapel -Libres en Cristo 10A-11A SCU—First Eve Free 11:30A-1:30P Old Chapel—Acts 13 2:00P—3:30P Christian Science 5:45P Old Chapel—Fruit of the Spirit	**21** 5:45P Sap4 Cause Community	**2022** 5:45P Sap4 Prison Fellowship Pre-Release/12 Steps	**23** 12:30P-1:30P SHU Chaplain Woodard 2P-3:30P Chapel Open Line Chaplain Woodard 5:45P Chapel— Chap Woodard
27 8:30A-11A Old Chapel Libres en Cristo 10A-12A SCU—Aglow Prison Ministry 11:30A-1:30P Old Chapel —The Rock Church 5:45P Old Chapel—On The Move	**28** 5:45P Sap4 Something Beautiful	**29** 5:45P Sap4 Prison Fellowship Pre-Release/12 Steps	**30** 12:30P-1:30P SCU Chap Woodard 5:45P Chapel Chap Woodard

Thu	Fri	Sat
3 5:45P Chapel -Chap Woodard 2:30P Harrison Spanish Choir 12:30P-1:30P PIP Chaplain Woodard 2:00-3:30 PM—Open Line Chaplain Woodard 5:45P SCU Christian Freedom 5:45P Old Chapel —On The Move	**4** 12:30P-1:30P C/C Chaplain Woodard 2P-3:30P Chapel—Open Line Chaplain Woodard 5:45P—Prison Fellowship Sap5—TUMI 5:45 P Old Chapel— Victory Outreach	**5** 1:30P-3:30P Old Chapel Choir 5:45P Rec Yard—Chosen Generation 5:45P SCU—Calvary Chapel Pacific Hills 5:45 P Old Chapel —Chaplain Woodard 5:45P-Old Chapel - Praise Dancer
10 2:30P Harrison -Spanish Choir 12:30P-1:30P CTC—Chap Woodard 2P-3:30P Chapel—Open Line Chaplain Woodard 5:45P SCU—Christian Freedom 5:45P Chapel— Chap Woodard 5:45P Old Chapel Jesus Is The Key	**11** 2P-3:30P-Chapel-Open Line-Chap Woodard 5:45P SAP4—Prison Fellowship TUMI 5:45P—Old Chapel—It's Almost Midnight	**12** 1:30P-3:30P-Old Chapel Choir 5:45 Rec Yard—Chosen Generation 5:45P Old Chapel—Lighthouse 5:45P—Chapel—Praise Dancers
17 12:30P-1:30P OPHU Chap Woodard 2P-3:30P Chapel Open Line-Chaplain Woodard 5:45P SCU Christian Freedom 5:45P Old Chapel Bible Enrichment 2:30P-Harrison -Spanish Choir 5:45P Chapel Chap Woodard	**18** 12:30P-1:30P SCU—Chaplain Woodard 2P-3:30P Chapel—Open Line Chaplain Woodard 5:45 P Old Chapel -Chaney Ministry 5:45 SAP4—Prison Fellowship TUMI	**19** 9A-11A —Later Day Saints/ Mormon/Chapel 1:30P-3:30P-Old Chapel—Choir 5:45 SCU—Calvary Pacific Hills 5:45P Old Chapel— Sixty One-One 5:45P—Chapel—Praise Dancers
24 12:30P-1:30P SCU Chap Woodard 2P-3:30P Chapel Open Line-Chaplain Woodard 5:45P SCU Christian Freedom 5:45P Old Chapel —Word of Fire 2:30P-Harrison -Spanish Choir 5:45P Chapel Chap Woodard	**25** 12:30P-1:30P SCU—Chaplain Woodard 2P-3:30P Chapel—Open Line Chap Woodard 5:45P Old Chapel —Gatekeepers 5:45P SAP4—Prison Fellowship TUMI	**26 TRT Auditorium 11:30A—3:30P** 5:45 Rec Yard—Chosen Generation 5:45P Old Chapel WLA COGIC 5:45P Chapel - Praise Dancers

* This is a photograph of the actual schedule that was sent to me by a friend still incarcerated at CIW.

Table 5: Rating Communication

Q#	Question Item	1	2	3	4	5		FIW Avg	PMV Avg	Diff
1	same					○ ▷	different	4.4	4.9	0.5
2	clear				○▷		unclear	3.5	3.8	0.3
3	warm			▷○			cold	2.9	2.8	-0.1
4	good			▷ ○			bad	3.3	2.8	-0.5
5	real			▷	○		fake	3.9	2.6	-1.3
6	understood			▷	○		misunderstood	4.1	3.3	-0.9
7	happy			▷○			sad	2.9	2.8	-0.1
8	fair			▷	○		unfair	3.5	2.6	-0.9
9	truth			▷○			lies	3.4	3.0	-0.4
10	family			▷	○		stranger	3.8	3.1	-0.7
11	connected			▷	○		unconnected	4.3	3.2	-1.1
12	strong			▷	○		weak	4.1	3.0	-1.1
13	wise			▷○			stupid	3.0	2.5	-0.5
14	spiritual			▷○			worldly	2.8	2.3	-0.5
15	godly			▷			ungodly	2.5	2.5	0.0
16	peaceful			○▷			stressful	2.7	2.8	0.1
17	easy			▷○			hard	3.3	3.1	-0.2
18	sober	○		▷			high	2.1	3.2	1.0
19	loving		▷○				hostile	2.2	2.2	0.0
20	inclusive			▷	○		exclusive	3.3	2.3	-1.0
		FIW – Circle		PMV - Triangle			Average	3.3	2.9	-0.4

Table 6: Perception of Personal Power

Q#	Question Item	FIW	PMV	Diff.
1	Female Correctional Officer	3.1	2.8	0.3
2	Male Doctor	2.6	2.4	0.1
3	Prison Chaplain	2.3	2.6	-0.4
4	Female Ministry Volunteer	2.8	3.4	-0.6
5	Hispanic Man	2.8	3.3	-0.5
6	Your Eldest Child	4.2	3.7	0.5
7	Your Best Friend	3.9	3.6	0.2
8	White Woman	3.0	3.5	-0.5
9	Short Termer Inmate	3.4	3.5	-0.1
10	Prison Warden	2.7	2.3	0.5
11	Male Correctional Officer	3.2	2.5	0.7
12	African-American Woman	3.2	3.2	0.0
13	White Man	3.4	3.6	-0.2
14	Long Termer/Lifer Inmate	3.7	3.2	0.5
15	Female Doctor	2.9	2.3	0.6
16	African-American Man	2.9	3.1	-0.2
17	Hispanic Woman	3.4	3.4	0.0
18	Male Ministry Volunteer	2.9	3.3	-0.4
19	Your Spouse	3.7	3.7	0.0
20	President Obama	1.8	2.2	-0.4

Bibliography

Allison, Maria T. and Dan Hibbler. 2004. "Organizational Barriers to Inclusion: Perspectives from the Recreation Professional." Leisure Sciences 26 (3):261-280. doi: 10.1080/01490400490461396.

Ardener, Shirley. 1975. "Introduction." In Perceiving Women, edited by Shirley Ardener. London: Malaby Press Limited.

Ardener, Shirley. 2005. "Ardener's "Muted Groups": The Genesis of an Idea and its Praxis: ." Women and Language 28 (2):50.

Barkman, Linda. 2017. "Towards a Missional Theology of Prison Ministry." International Journal of Pentecostal Missiology 5:38-53.

Bernard, H. Russell. 2011. Research Methods in Anthrolpology: Qualitative and Quantitative Approaches, fifth edition. NY, NY: Rowman & Littlefield.

Brown, Mark and Stuart Ross. 2010. "Mentoring, Social Capital and Desistance: A Study of Women Released from Prison." The Australian and New Zealand Journal of Criminology 43 (1):31-50.

Chadwick, Scott A. 1995. "Contexts of Communication." accessed 3/4/16. http://oregonstate.edu/instruct/theory/mutedgrp.html.

Colfer, Carol J. Pierce. 1982. "On communication Among "Unequals"." International Journal of Intercultural Relations 7 (3):263-283.

Dorodnych, Anatolij and Anna Kuzio. 2012. "The Role of Cultural Scripts and Contextualization Cues in Intercultural (Mis)communication." In Intercultural Miscommunication Past and Present, edited by Kryk-Kastovsky. Frankfurt, GE: Peter Lang, Internationaler Verlag der Wissenschaften.

Evangelization, Lausann Committee for World. 1978. "The Pasadena Consultation: Homogeneous Unit Principle." Lausanne Occasional Paper !, Pasadena, CA.

Fine, Michelle and Maria Elena Torre. 2006. "Intimate Details: Participatory Action Research in Prison." Action Research 4:253-269.

Greer, Kimberly. 2002. "Walking an Emotional Tightrope: Managing Emotions in a Women's Prison." Symbolic Interaction 25 (1):117-139.

Griffin, Brad M. 2012. "What is Urban Ministry." Fuller Youth Institute Blog, July, 13.

Heckathorn, Douglas D. 2011. "Snowball versus Respondent-Driven Sampling." Sociological Methodology 41 (1):355-366.

Hiebert, Paul G. 1978. "How much must Papayya 'know' about the Gospel to be Converted?" Gospel in Context 1 (4):24-29.

Hiebert, Paul G. 1994. Anthropological Reflections on Missiological Issues. Grand Rapids, MI: Baker Books.

Isasi-Diaz, Ada Maria. 2004. La Lucha Continues: Mujerista Theology. Maryknoll, NY: Orbis Books.

Johnson, Byron R. 2004. "Religious Programs and Recidivism Among Former Inmates in Prison Fellowship Programs: A Long-Term Follow-Up Study." Justice Quarterly 21 (2):329-354.

Johnson, Rachel. 2014. "Muted Group Theory – The Film." [YouTube]. https://www.youtube.com/watch?v=_beiMIQm_OA.

Johnston, Anne, Barbara Friedman, and Sara Peach. 2011. "Standpoint in Political Blogs: Voice, Authority, and Issues." Women's Studies 40 (3):269-298. doi: 10.1080/00497878.2010.548427.

Kann, Drew. 2019. 5 Facts Behind America's High Incarceration Rate. 2019. Accessed April 21, 2019.

Koschmann, Matthew A. and Brittany L. Peterson. 2013. "Rethinking Recidivism: A Communication Approach to Prisoner Reentry." Journal of Applied Social Science 7 (22):188-207.

Kramarae, Cheris. 1981. Women and Men Speaking: Frameworks for Analysis. Rowley, MA: Newbury House.

Kramarae, Cheris. 2005. "Muted Group Theory and Communication: Asking Dangerous Questions." Women and Language 28 (2):55-61.

Krolokke, Charlotte and Anne Scott Sorensen. 2006. Gender CommunicationTheories and Analyses: From Silence to Performance. Thousand Oaks, CA: Sage Publication.

Kvale, Steinar. 2007. Doing Interviews. Edited by Uwe Flick, The Sage Qualitative Research Kit. Los Angeles, CA: SAGE.

Leitzell, Carolyn, Natalie Madrazo, and Caren Warner-Robbins. 2011. "Meeting the Gap and Implications for Public Health Professionals." Home Health Care Management & Practice 23 (3):168-175.

Lepchitz, Rachel. 2012. "Perceived Muted Voice and its Impact on Female Communication Techniques in the Workplace." MA Unpublished Thesis, Communication and Leadership Studies, Gongaza University.

Lerman, Amy E. and Vesla M. Weaver. 2014. How Urban Policing and Mass Imprisonment Create a Second-Class Citizenship in America. Featured Research.

Mahoney, Annette M., and Carol Ann Daniel. 2008. "Bridging the Power Gap: Narrative Therapy with Incarcerated Women." The Prison Journal 86 (1):75-88.

McGavran, Donald A. 1990. Understanding Church Growth, 3rd Ed. Grand Rapids, MI: Wm. B. Eerdmans Publishing Co.

McLuhan, Marshall. 1964. Understanding Media: The Extensions of Man. Cambridge, MA: MIT Press.

Meares, Mary, Annette Torres, Denise Derkacs, John Oetzel, and Tamar Ginossar. 2004. "Employee mistreatment and muted voices in the culturally diverse workplace." Journal of Applied Communication Research 32 (1):4-27.

Mills, Jean. 2006. "Talking about silence: Gender and the construction of multilingual identities." International Journal of Bilingualism 10 (1):1-16. doi: 10.1177/13670069060100010101.

Morani, Nicole M. Nora Wikoff, Donald M. Linhorst, and Sheila Bratton. 2011. "A Description of the Self-Identified Needs, Service Expenditures, and Social Outcomes of Participants of a Prisoner-Reentry Program." The Prison Journal 91 (3):347-365.

Mutua, Consolata Nthemba. 2014. "Opposite Worlds, Singular Mission: Teaching as an ITA." New Directions for Teaching & Learning 2014 (138):51-60. doi: 10.1002/tl.20096.

Neuliep, James. 2017. Intercultural Communication: A Contextual Approach 7th ed.

Thousand Oaks, CA: Sage.

O'Connor Tom P, and Jeff B. Duncan. 2011. "The Sociology of Humanist, Spiritual, and religious Practice in Prison: Supporting Responsivity and Desistance from Crime." Religions 2:590-610.

Olson, Roger E. 2007. Reformed and Always Reforming: The Postconservative Approach to Evangelical Theology. Grand Rapids, MI: Baker Academic.

Orbe, Mark P. 2005. "Continuing the Legacy of Theorizing From the Margins: Conceptualizations of Co-Cultural Theory." Women and Language 28 (2):65-66,72.

Owen, Barbara A. 1998. In The Mix. Albany, NY: SUNY Press.

Sexton, Jason S. 2015. "Toward a prison theology of California's ecclesia incarcerate." Theology 118 (2):83-91. doi: 10.1177/0040571x14559159.

Shaw, R. Daniel 2002. "Three-Day Visitors: The Samo Response to Colonialism in Western Province, Papua New Guinea." In Colonial New Guinea: Anthropological Perspectives, edited by Naomi McPherson. Pittsburgh, PA: University of Pittsburgh Press.

Thomas, Dorothy Q.; Deborah Blatt; Robin S. Levi; Sarah Lai; Joanne Mariner; and Regan E. Ralph. 1996. "All Too Familiar: Sexual Abuse of Women in U.S. State Prisons." Human Rights Watch (December 1996).

Vasanta, D. 2001. "Researching Language and Gender: A Critical Review." Indian Journal of Gender Studies 8 (1):69-87. doi: 10.1177/097152150100800104.

Vuolo, Mike and Candace Kruttschitt. 2008. "Prisoners' Adjustment, Correctional Officers, and Context: The Foreground and Background of Punishment in Late Modernity." Law and Society Review 42 (2):307-336.

Wall, Celia J. and Pat Gannon-Leary 1999. "A Sentence Made by Men: Muted Group Theory Revisited." European Journal of Women's Studies 6 (1):21-29.

West, Richard L. and Lynn H. Turner. 2004. "Introducing Communication Theory: Analysis and Application, 2nd Ed." In: McGraw-Hill Higher Education Online Resources (accessed 1/29/16).

Wood, Julia T. 2005. "Feminist Standpoint Theory and Muted Group Theory: Commonalities and Divergences." Women and Language 28 (2):61-65.

Yoder, Michael L., Michael H. Lee, Jonathan Ro, Robert J. Priest. 2009. "Understand Christian Identity in Terms of Bounded and Centered Set Theory in the Writings of Paul G. Hiebert." Trinity Journal 30 (2):177-188.

www.ingramcontent.com/pod-product-compliance
Lightning Source LLC
Chambersburg PA
CBHW050552160426
43199CB00015B/2629